D0451745

Invoking the Spirit

RELIGION AND SPIRITUALITY IN THE QUEST FOR A SUSTAINABLE WORLD

GARY GARDNER

Jane Peterson, *Editor*

WORLDWATCH PAPER 164

December 2002

THE WORLDWATCH INSTITUTE is an independent research organization that works for an environmentally sustainable and socially just society, in which the needs of all people are met without threatening the health of the natural environment or the well-being of future generations. By providing compelling, accessible, and fact-based analysis of critical global issues, Worldwatch informs people around the world about the complex interactions between people, nature, and economies. Worldwatch focuses on the underlying causes of and practical solutions to the world's problems, in order to inspire people to demand new policies, investment patterns, and lifestyle choices.

FINANCIAL SUPPORT for the Institute is provided by the Ford Foundation, the Richard & Rhoda Goldman Fund, the George Gund Foundation, the William and Flora Hewlett Foundation, The Frances Lear Foundation, the Steve Leuthold Foundation, the Charles Stewart Mott Foundation, the Curtis and Edith Munson Foundation, the John D. and Catherine T. MacArthur Foundation, the Overbrook Foundation, the David and Lucile Packard Foundation, the Surdna Foundation, Inc., the Turner Foundation, Inc., UN Environment Programme, the Wallace Global Fund, the Weeden Foundation, and the Winslow Foundation. The Institute also receives financial support from its Council of Sponsors members—Adam and Rachel Albright, Tom and Cathy Crain, and Robert Wallace and Raisa Scriabine—and from the many other friends of Worldwatch.

THE WORLDWATCH PAPERS provide in-depth, quantitative, and qualitative analysis of the major issues affecting prospects for a sustainable society. The Papers are written by members of the Worldwatch Institute research staff and reviewed by experts in the field. They have been used as concise and authoritative references by governments, nongovernmental organizations, and educational institutions worldwide. For a partial list of available Worldwatch Papers, see back pages.

REPRINT AND COPYRIGHT INFORMATION for one-time academic use of this material is available by contacting Customer Service, Copyright Clearance Center, at (978) 750-8400 (phone), or (978) 750-4744 (fax), or writing to CCC, 222 Rosewood Drive, Danvers, MA 01923. Nonacademic users should call the Worldwatch Institute's Business Development Department at (202) 452-1992, x520, or fax a request to (202) 296-7365.

© Worldwatch Institute, 2002

ISBN 1-878071-67-X

Library of Congress Control Number: 2002115545

❀ Printed on paper that is 100 percent recycled, 100 percent post-consumer waste, process chlorine free.

The views expressed are those of the author and do not necessarily represent those of the Worldwatch Institute; of its directors, officers, or staff; or of its funding organizations.

GU
185.7
637
2002

Table of Contents

ACKNOWLEDGEMENTS: I am indebted to a supportive network of people for constructive critiques of this paper. Feedback from the Institute's entire research and communications staff on an early draft was instrumental in steering the project in a new and more effective direction. I am especially indebted to Erik Assadourian for his tireless efforts to dig up obscure information, and for his ongoing feedback and brainstorming on approaches to this sensitive topic. Kelly Alley, Maria Becket, John Bennett, Cassandra Carmichael, Richard Foltz, and Fran Peavey also gave helpful critiques. Mary Evelyn Tucker and John Grim were exceedingly generous not only with review comments, but also with guidance to the topic of religion and ecology in general. Jane Peterson helped broaden and balance the paper's argument and patiently untangled my knotty prose. Joan Wolbier did a quick and accurate job on the layout; Lisa Mastny was masterful in proofreading; and Leanne Mitchell, Dick Bell, Susanne Martikke, and Susan Finkelpearl of the Institute's Communications Department were superb in getting the word out about the paper. Finally, I am indebted to Sally Gardner for her encouragement to pursue this project. It was a constant and greatly appreciated source of strength.

GARY GARDNER is Director of Research at Worldwatch. His research has spanned a broad range of issues, from cropland loss and malnutrition to materials use and social change. Since joining the Institute in 1994, he has authored eight chapters in the Institute's annual *State of the World* report, and authored or co-authored six Worldwatch Papers.

   Before joining the Institute, Gary was project manager of the Soviet Nonproliferation Project, a research and training program run by the Monterey Institute of International Studies (MIIS) in California. There he authored *Nuclear Nonproliferation: A Primer*, which is also published in Spanish and Russian. Gary holds Master's degrees in Politics from Brandeis University, and in Public Administration from MIIS, and a Bachelor's degree from Santa Clara University. He is fluent in Spanish.

Summary

The effort to build a sustainable world could advance dramatically if religious people and institutions, on one hand, and environmentalists and advocates of sustainable development, on the other, were to embrace each other's central concerns. But to do so, the longstanding distrust between the two communities would need to be overcome.

The two groups share important interests. Each looks at the world from a moral perspective; each views nature as having value that surpasses economics; and each opposes excessive consumption. They also have complementary strengths. Advocates of sustainability are strongly rooted in science, and have a concrete vision for sustainability. Religious traditions enjoy moral authority and a broad grassroots presence that puts them in a powerful position to shape the worldviews and lifestyles of billions of people.

Religions possess one or more of five sources of power. They shape people's worldviews, wield moral authority, have the ear of multitudes of adherents, often possess strong financial and institutional assets, and are strong generators of social capital, an asset in community building. All of these assets can be used to help build a socially just and environmentally sustainable world.

In the 1990s, interactions between environmental and religious groups increased in frequency and importance. International meetings, national networks of interreligious activism, religiously sponsored environmental advocacy and education programs, collaborations between religious and environmental groups, and grassroots religious and environmental advocacy are examples of the many initiatives that blossomed over the decade.

At the same time, barriers that have prevented collaboration in the past will need to be surmounted if the two communities are to get together. Mutual misperceptions and divergent worldviews are at the root of most issues that separate them. In particular, concern over the checkered history of religious involvement in societal affairs, and divergent perspectives on the role of women, the nature of truth, and the moral status of humanity in the natural order have posed obstacles to cooperation. But none of these differences need prevent collaboration on the many areas of interest common to the two groups.

Several examples of engagement of environmental issues by religious people demonstrate how religious people and organizations are wielding their power to help build a sustainable world. The Ecumenical Patriarch Bartholomew uses his moral authority to gather prominent scientists, journalists, and religious leaders for week-long, on-site symposia focusing on water-related environmental issues. Environmentalist monks in Thailand have employed their moral authority, along with ritual, to preserve forests in that country. And activists trying to prevent abuse of the Ganges River in India carefully consider and respect the divergent secular and Hindu worldviews.

On the consumption front, religions are also active in various ways. Most religions in industrial countries are more active in urging congregations to shift consumption to "green" products, such as fair-traded coffee, than they are in promoting reduction in consumption. In one developing country, however—Sri Lanka—the Sarvodaya Shramadana movement is actively promoting a Buddhist-inspired vision of development that includes an ethic of moderate consumption.

To further the engagement of environmentalism and spirit, religious people and institutions would do well to consider applying their strong assets to the pursuit of sustainability. Environmentalists, meanwhile, would gain by opening to the rich spiritual dimensions of environmentalism, recognizing that

they need to do more to appeal to the public on an emo-
tional/spiritual level. If both sides can take these steps, a new
ethics, encompassing not only humans and the divine, but
nature as well, can be developed to establish a just and sustainable civilization.

Introduction

A s the U.S. debate over drilling for oil in Alaska's Arctic
National Wildlife Refuge (ANWR) gathered steam in early
2002, an unusual ad appeared on television. Over magnificent
shots of seacoasts, forests, and mountains, the narrator intones
a Jewish prayer in which God says, "This is a beautiful world
I have given you. Take care of it; do not ruin it." The ad then
argues against drilling in ANWR and proposes that America's
energy needs be met through conservation, higher fuel efficiency standards, and greater use of solar and wind power. Perhaps the most arresting statement is the last one: "Brought to
you by the Sierra Club and the National Council of Churches."[1]

The teaming of a prominent U.S. environmental organization and a coalition of mainline Christian churches is especially surprising because environmentalists and people of faith
have had limited contact since the start of the modern environmental movement. Nevertheless, it may represent an
emerging trend, for spiritual traditions—from large, centralized
religions to local tribal spiritual authorities—are beginning
to devote energy to what some see as the defining challenge
of our age: the need to build just and environmentally healthy
societies. Worldwide, the major faiths are issuing declarations,
advocating new national policies, and designing educational
activities in support of a sustainable world, sometimes in partnership with secular environmental organizations such as the
Sierra Club, sometimes on their own. Responding to the global
crisis, smaller traditions are reviving ancient rituals and practices in the service of sustainability. The quickening of religious
interest in environmental issues suggests that a powerful new

political alignment may be emerging, one that could greatly strengthen the effort to build a sustainable world.

A strong set of common interests inspires this tentative engagement of the spiritual and sustainability communities and would appear to make them natural allies. Both look at the world from a moral perspective, stressing obligations that extend beyond the individual to other people, distant places, and future generations. Both generally see the natural world as having value that transcends economics. And both oppose the excessive consumption that drives industrial economies. Moreover, the two groups have complementary strengths. Advocates of sustainability have strong scientific grounding and a concrete vision, while religious traditions enjoy moral authority and an extensive grassroots presence that puts them in a powerful position to shape the worldview and lifestyles of billions of people. It was recognition of these compatibilities that led to the unusual partnership on ANWR. It also prompted the government of Pakistan to turn to Muslim clergy for environmental education, and inspired the symbolic leader of the world's roughly 250 million adherents to the Greek and other national Orthodox churches to bring religious leaders and scientists together for on-site environmental symposia, to name just a few examples.[2]

The budding rapprochement of religious and environmental groups could be of historical significance. Should it blossom, it could help to heal the centuries-old rift in the West between religion and the sciences (including economics and other social sciences). These two streams of thought, especially in the West, have diverged since the European enlightenment, with science gradually replacing religion as the authoritative source for some of humanity's most profound questions, such as how the universe was formed. In the process, however, the scientific focus on writing an objective story about "what is" was achieved largely without reference to the emotive story of "what ought to be," a traditional strength of religion. By the twentieth century, industrial societies in particular were strongly oriented to the cognitive, the rational, and the logical, with devastating consequences: science largely unrestrained by ethics (whether from religion or anywhere else) helped to deliver the most violent and most environmentally damaging century in human history. (See Box 1.)[3]

One corollary of this evolution is that development—at its simplest, the effort to improve the quality of people's lives—became associated more and more exclusively with advances in material well-being, as if the human spirit were only incidental to individual and societal betterment. Development programs tended to focus on building infrastructure and improving human health and welfare—a necessary but incomplete agenda that suffered from its tendency to ignore crucial cultural factors or at best to give them insufficient attention. The material focus of development reached an extreme in industrial nations in the 20th century, as ever-spiraling levels of production and consumption became the goal of most economics ministries. Mass consumption offered compelling, but ultimately unsatisfying answers to the deepest questions asked by human beings. Whereas religions saw enlightenment or the effort to love, for example, as our purpose in life, the consumer culture said our purpose was maximizing pleasure, and proclaimed that more is better than less; new is better than used; resources are essentially infinite. These and other articles of economic faith can shape the worldview, ethics, and behaviors of a society as much as the precepts of any religion. Indeed, some critics today argue that market capitalism, with its attempt to deliver happiness, represents a strong challenge to the influence of the world's established religions.[4]

Without a spiritual counterbalance, the material emphasis in modern thinking about development may actually be detrimental to the personal and societal betterment it purports to bring about. One example of this is found in the increasingly poor eating habits in industrial nations, where overconsumption of pleasurable fatty and sugary foods has generated enormous profits for corporations while at the same time producing alarming rates of obesity and a growing epidemic of diabetes and other serious health conditions, thereby incurring costs that represent a clear step backward for indi-

BOX 1

What Is Religion, and How Is it Relevant to the Environment?

A single, authoritative definition of religion remains elusive, despite religion's status as one of the oldest human institutions. Still, several characteristics common to many definitions can help stake out its boundaries. In the most general terms, religion is an orientation to the cosmos and to our role in it. It offers people a sense of ultimate meaning and the possibility for personal transformation and celebration of life. To this end it uses a range of resources, including worldviews, symbols, rituals, ethical norms, traditions, and (sometimes) institutional structures. Religion also offers a means of experiencing a sustaining creative force, whether a creator deity, an awe-inspiring presence in nature, or simply the source of all life.

Many of these characteristics give religion substantial influence over the environment. Worldviews shape attitudes toward the natural world; rituals have been used to govern resource use, especially among indigenous peoples; ethics influences resource use and distribution; and institutional power can shape behaviors and policies in ways that affect the environment, for better or worse.

Source: See endnote 3.

vidual and societal development. Barring spiritual sanction against excessive consumption, and the ethical sanction against the economic forces that promote it (such as junk food ads targeted at children), this undermining of development can be expected to continue unchecked.[5]

A major challenge for our civilization is to reintegrate our societal heart and head, to reestablish spirituality as a partner in dialogue with science. This will require the world's religious traditions to intensify their engagement of environmental and developmental issues. It will also require that development and environmental organizations build on their openness to the spiritual dimensions of sustainability, as the Sierra Club has done. To accomplish this rapprochement, the two groups will need to surmount the suspicion and misunderstanding that have kept them at arm's length for at least 30 years.

Each community has strong incentives to expand engagement. For people of faith, environmental issues offer an opportunity to raise their profile and gain new societal relevance and respect by addressing one of the most critical issues of our time. Many religions also have well-honed expertise in some elements of the sustainable development agenda, boasting in particular a long history of teaching against excessive attachment to material goods and a track record in favor of social justice. Environmentalists, who constitute a relatively new social movement, would benefit from allying with a huge and active constituency. Given the numbers of religious people in the world today, such a joining of forces could have far-reaching impacts.

For the two communities to come together will require a certain amount of humility on both sides. The checkered history of religious involvement in societal affairs—multiple episodes of warfare, oppression, intolerance, and hypocrisy—is commonly cited by environmentalists as a reason to avoid engagement with religion, even by those who acknowledge the admirable selflessness and the passionate defense of marginalized people that are a major part of religious history. At the same time, the environmental community has often alienated potential allies with what is perceived as a narrow-minded right eousness. It needs to recognize that culture is central to national development—and that religion is central to most cultures. In other words, environmentalists would do well to appreciate that a sustainable world cannot be built without full engagement of the human spirit. With great effort, the two communities could indeed bring about a historic reconciliation and generate the societal energy needed to sustain the planet and its people.[6]

The Potential Power of Engaged Religion

Religious institutions and leaders can bring at least five strong assets to the effort to build a sustainable world: the capacity to shape cosmologies (worldviews); moral authority; a large base of adherents; significant material resources; and community-building capacity. Religions are experienced at informing our perspectives on issues of ultimate concern.

They know how to inspire people and how to wield moral authority. Many have the political clout associated with a huge base of adherents. Some have considerable real estate holdings, buildings, and financial resources. And most produce strong community ties by generating social resources such as trust and cooperation, which can be a powerful boost to community development. Many political movements would welcome any of these five assets. To be endowed with most or all of them, as many religions are, is to wield considerable political power.

Indeed, religion is an important source of change within individuals and across societies. Cultural historian Thomas Berry sees religion, along with education, business, and government, as the major societal drivers of change in the world. And a recent textbook on psychology and the natural environment lists religion as one of four key sources of individual behavior change throughout history. Indeed, major societal changes of recent decades support these assertions. The Nicaraguan revolution (which was strongly backed by proponents of "liberation theology"), the U.S. Civil Rights movement led by the Reverend Martin Luther King and energized by thousands of religious supporters, and the Shi'ite-inspired Iranian revolution are just a few societal-level changes in the twentieth century that were strongly influenced or led by religious institutions or people of faith. Meanwhile, the global boycott of Nestlé products in the 1970s is an example of individual (consumer) behavior change that was bolstered by religious groups.[7]

The first key asset that religion brings to bear on societal change is the capacity to provide meaning by shaping one's cosmology, or worldview—the fundamental philosophical grounding out of which a person lives his or her life. A cosmology offers answers to the most profound questions human beings ask: Who am I? Why am I here? What are my obligations to the world around me? Cosmologies are typically expressed in the form of stories—tools of communication that engage people at a deep emotional level. The creation stories of many religious traditions, for example, offer ways of interpreting not only the origin of the universe, but peoples' place and purpose in it as well. Thus, cosmologies give rise to ethics, because they help people to understand their relationship with each other and, in some traditions, their relationship to the natural world. The capacity to influence cosmology, therefore, translates into influence over ethics, and in turn, influence over behavior.[8]

Religious cosmologies regarding the natural environment are diverse, and the broad range of teachings might suggest that some religions are naturally "greener" than others. But the reality is more complex. Nearly all religions can be commended and criticized for one aspect or another of their posture toward the environment. A religion's environmental credentials may depend on whether its teaching, its practice, or its potential for "greening" itself is being assessed. And scholars see great potential for developing environmental ethics even within traditions that have not emphasized them. (See Box 2.)[9]

Religion's capacity to provide meaning is rooted deep in the human psyche. This capacity is often expressed through symbols, rituals, myths, and other practices that work at the level of affect. These speak to us from a primal place, a place where we "know" in a subconscious way. Ritual, for example—the repeated patterns of activity that carry the often inexpressible meaning of human experience—is a deep form of communication that is tapped by both religious and secular leaders. A president or prime minister singing the national anthem at a sporting event, hand over heart, is engaging in a powerful ritualistic behavior that speaks to compatriots in a profound way. Needing tools to express spiritual concepts that are well beyond the capacity of language to convey, religious and spiritual traditions for millennia have turned to ritual for help.[10]

Ritual communication, it turns out, has also had an important role in environmental protection among traditional societies. Where resources have been managed well, the credit often goes to "religious or ritual representation of resource management," according to cultural ecologist E. N.

BOX 2

Selected Religious Perspectives on Nature

In the three western monotheistic traditions—Judaism, Christianity, and Islam—morality has traditionally been human-focused, with nature being of secondary importance and with God transcending the natural world. Thus, the natural world can be seen as a set of resources for human use, a perspective that some observers blame for the wasteful and destructive development of the past two centuries. Yet scholars in each of these traditions find substantial grounds for building a strong environmental ethics. The Judaic concept of a covenant or legal agreement between God and humanity, for example, can be extended to all of creation. The Christian focus on sacrament and incarnation are seen as lenses through which the entire natural world can be viewed as sacred. And the Islamic concept of vice-regency teaches that the natural world is not owned by humans but is given to them in trust—a trust that implies certain responsibilities to preserve the balance of creation.

Hinduism and Buddhism in South Asia contain teachings concerning the natural world that are arguably in conflict. Some scholars in these traditions emphasize the illusory nature of the material world and the desirability of escaping suffering by turning to a timeless world of spirit, in the case of Hinduism, or by seeking release in nirvana, in the case of some meditative schools of Buddhism. This other-worldly orientation, some scholars argue, minimizes the importance of environmental degradation. On the other hand, both religions place great emphasis on correct conduct and on fulfillment of duty, which often includes obligations to environmental preservation. Thus, Hindus regard rivers as sacred, and in the concept of *lila*, the creative play of the gods, Hindu theology engages the world as a creative manifestation of the divine. Meanwhile, Buddhist environmentalists often stress the importance of trees in the life of the Buddha, and "socially engaged" Buddhism in Asia and the United States is active in environmental protection, especially of forests. Moreover, the Mahayana schools of Buddhism emphasize the interdependent nature of reality in such images as the jeweled net of Indra, in which each jewel reflects all the others in the universe.

The East Asian traditions of Confucianism and Taoism seamlessly link the divine, human, and natural worlds. The divine is not seen as transcendent; instead, the Earth's fecundity is seen as continuously unfolding through nature's movements across the seasons and through human workings in the cycles of agriculture. This organic worldview is centered around the concept of ch'i, the dynamic, material force that infuses the natural and human worlds, unifying matter and spirit. Confucianists and Taoists seek to live in harmony with nature and with other human beings, while paying attention to the movements of the Tao, the Way. Despite the affinity of these traditions with an environmental ethic, however, deforestation, pollution, and other forms of environmental degradation have become widespread in contemporary East Asia due to many factors, including rapid industrialization and the decline of traditional

Box 2 (continued)

values in the last 50 years with the spread of Communism.

Finally, indigenous traditions, closely tied to their local bioregion for food and for materials for clothing, shelter, and cultural activities, tend to have their environmental ethics embedded in their worldviews. Gratitude for the fecundity of nature is a common feature of their cultures. Ritual calendars are often derived from the cycles of nature, such as the appearance of the sun or moon, or the seasonal return of certain animals or plants. Indigenous traditions often have a very light environmental footprint compared with industrial societies. Still, many indigenous traditions recall times of environmental degradation in their mythologies. Since the colonial period, the efforts of indigenous people to live sustainably in their homelands have been hurt by the encroachment of settlements and by logging, mining, and other forms of resource exploitation.

Source: See endnote 9.

Anderson. Before stripping bark from cedar trees, for instance, the Tlingit Indians of the Pacific Northwest perform a ritual apology to the spirits they believe live there, promising to take only what they need. Among the Tsembaga people of New Guinea, pig festivals, ritual pig slaughters, and pig-eating rituals play a key role in maintaining ecological balance, redistributing land and pigs among people, and ensuring that the neediest are the first to receive limited supplies of pork. Rituals such as these are often dismissed as superstition by modern peoples, yet anthropologists assert that skilled use of ritual has made many traditional societies far more successful in caring for their environment than industrial societies have been. The key, says Anderson, is traditional societies' understanding that ritual helps people forge emotional connections with the natural world, connections that industrial societies are slow to make.[11]

Growing out of religion's capacity to shape worldviews is a second asset, the capacity to inspire, and the wielding of moral authority. It is a subtle asset, easily overlooked and often underestimated. Asked in 1935 if the Pope might prove to be an ally of the Soviet Union, Josef Stalin is said to have replied scornfully, "The Pope? How many divisions has he got?" The dictator's response betrays a dim understanding of the power that accrues to persons and organizations skilled in appealing to the depths of the human spirit. Ironically, papal influence exercised through the Solidarity protest movement in Poland in the early 1980s was an important factor in the eventual unraveling of Communist rule in Eastern Europe. Similarly, the Dalai Lama strongly affects Chinese government policy toward Tibet, even though he has lived in exile since 1959. Charisma and moral suasion are not the exclusive reserve of religious leaders, of course, but religious leaders have extensive experience in spiritual matters, and understand well the power inherent in touching people at the level of spirit.[12]

Turning to the more worldly assets, a third source of power for religions is the sheer numbers of followers they claim. Although the data are estimates, it seems that some 80–90 percent of people on the planet belong to one of 10,000 or so religions, and that 150 or so of these faith traditions have at least a million followers each. Adherents of the three largest—Christianity, Islam, and Hinduism—account for about two thirds of the global population today. Another 20 percent of the world's people subscribe to the remaining religions, and about 15 percent are nonreligious. (See Table 1.)[13]

Degrees of adherence among the billions of religious people vary greatly, of course, as does the readiness of adherents to translate their faith into political action or lifestyle choices. And many believers within the same religion or denomination may interpret their faith in conflicting ways, leading them to act at cross-purposes. But the raw numbers are so impressive that mobilizing even a fraction of adherents to the cause of building a just and environmentally healthy society could advance the sustainability agenda dramatically. Adding nonreligious but spiritually oriented people to the totals boosts the potential for influence even more.

Influence stemming from having a large number of followers is further enhanced by the geographic concentration of many religions, which increases their ability to make mass appeals and to coordinate action. In 120 countries, for example, Christians form the majority of the population. Muslims are the majority in 45 countries, as are Buddhists in nine.

TABLE 1

Major Religions: Number of Adherents and Share of World Population

Religion	Adherents in 2000 (million)	Share of World Population (percent)
Christianity	2,000	33.0
Islam	1,188	19.6
Hinduism	752	12.4
Confucianism and Chinese Folk Religion	391	6.5
Buddhism	360	5.9
Indigenous religions	228	3.8
Sikhism	23	0.4
Judaism	14	0.2
Spiritualism	12	0.2
Bahá'í Faith	7	0.1
Jainism	4	0.1
Shintoism	3	0.05
Taoism	3	0.05
Zoroastrianism	3	0.05
Total	4,988	82.40

Source: See endnote 13.

When most people in a society have similar worldviews, leaders can make mass appeals using a single, values-laden language. Pakistan did this in 2001 when, as a result of the National Conservation Strategy, the government enlisted Muslim clergy in the North West Frontier Province to launch an environmental awareness campaign based on teachings from the Qu'ran. Government leaders and nongovernmental organizations (NGOs) saw the religious leaders as a critical part of the campaign, given their broad presence in the country and the fact that in some regions more people go to mosques than to schools.[14]

Of course, size is not always the most important determinant of the potential to help shape a sustainable world.

Indigenous traditions, typically small in number, often possess great wisdom on how to live in harmony with nature. Most have an intimate knowledge of their local bioregion, which in turn is the source of revelation, ritual, and collective memory for them. And their worldviews tend to integrate the temporal and spiritual realms. Although the stereotype of indigenous people as good stewards of their resource base is overstated, specialists in religion and ecology see indigenous cultures as having rituals of reciprocity and respect for nature that enable them to leave an especially small environmental impact. These characteristics give them particular moral relevance that can be an important source of knowledge and inspiration in building a sustainable world.[15]

In some countries, the broad base of adherents coincides with a receptivity, if not yet a commitment, to issues of sustainability, which further increases religion's potential contribution to building a sustainable world. In a survey of Americans by the Biodiversity Project in Wisconsin, for example, 56 percent of respondents said that environmental protection is important because Earth is "God's creation." The Sierra Club's appreciation for the religious sensibilities of a broad swath of the American public led it to collaborate with the National Council of Churches on the television ads about the Arctic National Wildlife Refuge.[16]

The fourth asset that many religions can bring to the effort to build a sustainable world is substantial physical and financial resources. Real estate holdings alone are impressive. The Alliance for Religion and Conservation, an NGO based in the United Kingdom, estimates that religions own up to 7 percent of the land area of many countries. And buildings abound: Pakistan has one mosque for every 30 households; the United States has one house of worship for every 900 residents. In addition, clinics, schools, orphanages, and other social institutions run by religious organizations give them a network of opportunities to shape development efforts. A large share of schools are run by religious groups, especially in developing countries. Confucian and Indian Vedic health care make important contributions to the health systems of China and India. And in the

United States, the largest provider of social services after the federal government is the Catholic Church.[17]

While headlines regularly expose the less than ethical use of religious wealth, some exemplary cases illustrate the impact that religious institutions could have in helping to nudge the world toward sustainability. In the United States, the Interfaith Center for Corporate Responsibility (ICCR), representing 275 Protestant, Catholic, and Jewish institutional investors, has been a leader for more than three decades in shaping corporate operating policies through the use of social policy shareholder resolutions. More than half of all socially oriented shareholder resolutions initiated in the United States in the past three years were filed or co-filed by religious groups; on more than a third of them, religious groups were the primary filers. This role has caught the attention of secular activists on corporate responsibility. "One of the first things we do when we run a campaign is make sure that the ICCR is on board," says Tracey Rembert of the Shareholder Action Network, which advocates ethical investing and shareholder action.[18]

Finally, religion has a particular capacity to generate social capital: the bonds of trust, communication, cooperation, and information dissemination that create strong communities. Development economists began to recognize in the 1970s and 1980s that economic development is fueled not just by stocks of land, labor, and financial capital but also by education (human capital) and healthy ecosystems (ecological capital). By the 1990s, many theorists added social capital (community building) to the list because of its importance as a lubricant and glue in many communities: it greases the wheels of communication and interaction, which in turn strengthen the bonds that community members have with one another.[19]

While social capital is built by a broad range of groups in civil society, from political parties to civic clubs and hobby groups, religion is especially influential. Religions are present throughout most societies, including in the most remote rural areas. They tend to bring people together frequently, and they encourage members to help one another as well as the dispossessed. Perhaps most important, the beliefs shared among members are an especially strong unifying force. "Sacred meaning is one of the deepest bonding forces societies possess," notes Mary Clark, a writer on historical change. Moreover, she adds, where sacred meaning is absent, societies tend to disintegrate.[20]

Data from the United States support this interpretation of religion as community builder. Analyzing survey data, sociologist Andrew Greeley showed that religious institutions or persons, who are responsible for 34 percent of all volunteerism in the United States, fielded volunteers not just for religious work but for other society-building efforts as well. About a third of the educational, political, youth, and human services voluntarism, about a quarter of the health-related voluntarism, and about a fifth of the employment-related volunteer work was undertaken by people motivated by their faith. The willingness to work for societal betterment, not just for the particular interests of a religious group, holds potential for the movement to build a sustainable world, especially because the environment is an issue of common concern for the planet and for future generations that transcends religious and national differences.[21]

Cooperation and Caution

As deforestation, climate change, water shortages, extensive poverty, and other global ills have assumed greater prominence in the public mind, and as the religious and environmental communities increasingly appreciate their common interest in combating these problems, the two communities have begun to engage each other on the agenda of sustainable development. The trend is encouraging, and could represent the budding emergence of a powerful new alliance for sustainability. But significant obstacles to cooperation exist, and these must be managed well if the full engagement of environmentalists and believers is to be realized.

On the positive side, the pace of meetings and collaborations among religious and environmental groups has
increased markedly since the World Wide Fund for Nature
(WWF) sponsored an interreligious meeting in Assisi, Italy,
in 1986 that brought together representatives of five of the
world's major religions. That seminal meeting was followed
by other major conferences and initiatives, both between the
two communities and among religious traditions. (See Table
2.) Some of the initiatives have blossomed into networks. The
National Religious Partnership for the Environment in the
United States and the Alliance for Religions and Conservation in the United Kingdom, for example, bring together
diverse faith groups to plan strategies for raising awareness
and taking action on environmental issues. The increased
activity and commitment represented by the initiatives suggests that environmentalism is not just a passing interest for
religious groups.[22]

One development of particular note was the 10-part
conference series on world religions and ecology held at Harvard University's Center for the Study of World Religions
from 1996 to 1998. The series brought together the most
diverse spectrum of individuals and institutions ever con-
vened to discuss the topic, with more than 800 scholars and
environmental activists from major religious traditions, and
from six continents, participating. The conferences are note-
worthy not only for the scholarship they produced—nine
volumes on environmentalism from the perspective of major
religious traditions, with another forthcoming—but also for
their extensive engagement of people from outside of religion
and religious studies. Scientists, ethicists, educators, and public policy makers all took active part in the conference dia-
logues. A culminating conference was held at the American
Museum of Natural History, and the United Nations Environment Programme (UNEP) hosted conference organizers
for the press conference announcing their findings. Perhaps
most significant for the religion/environment dialogue, the
Forum on Religion and Ecology (the follow-on organization
to the conferences) is housed at Harvard's Center on the

TABLE 2

Religious Initiatives and Partnerships on Environment and Sustainability

Initiatives	Description
Worldwide Fund for Nature (WWF) conference Assisi, Italy, 1986	In the first major meeting of its kind, representatives of five of the world's major faiths discuss strategies for helping their communities to assist in protecting the environment.
World Council of Churches Climate Change Programme, 1999	The WCC creates a program to lobby governments and international organizations to fundamentally reorient "the socioeconomic structures and personal lifestyles" that have led to the current climate change crisis.
Global Forum of Spiritual and Parliamentary Leaders, 1988, 1990, 1992, and 1993	In their 1990 statement, 32 globally renowned scientists appeal to the world religious community "to commit, in word and deed, and boldly as is required, to preserve the environment of the Earth."
Parliament of World Religions, 1993 and 1999	Commemorating the first Parliament in 1893, representatives of the world's religions gather and issue declarations on ethics regarding global issues, from environmental degradation to violations of human rights.
Summit on Religion and Environment, Windsor, England, 1995	Hosted by Prince Phillip, leaders of nine world religions, along with secular leaders, gather to discuss implementation plans for religion-based conservation projects. The conference results in the creation of the Alliance of Religions and Conservation.
Harvard conferences on Religions of the World and Ecology, 1996–98	Some 800 scholars from a broad range of religious traditions do research and outreach work on the religion/ecology connection. Nine volumes, each focusing on a different tradition, are published. The Forum on Religion and Ecology emerges to continue the work.
Religion, Science and Environment Symposia, 1994, 1997, 1999, 2002	Ecumenical Patriarch Bartholomew convenes a series of shipboard symposia focusing on regional water-related environmental issues. The symposia involve scientists, policymakers, religious leaders, and journalists.
World Faiths Development Dialogue, London, 1998	A collaborative initiative between development institutions and nine world religions is organized under the leadership of the World Bank and the Archbishop of Canterbury. The initiative incorporates a spiritual voice into shaping the policies and practices of human development organizations.

Table 2 (continued)

Millennium World Peace Summit of Religious and Spiritual leaders, August 2000	More than 1,000 religious leaders meet at the United Nations; environment is a major topic of discussion. U.N. Secretary-General Kofi Annan calls for a new ethic of global stewardship.
Sacred Gifts for a Living Planet Conference, Nepal, 2000	Organized by WWF and ARC, 11 major religions, representing 4.5 billion people, offer 26 conservation gifts to help improve the environment.
International Seminar on Religion, Culture, and Environment, Tehran, June 2001	Sponsored by the United Nations Environment Programme and the Islamic Republic of Iran, the conference discusses the importance of fighting environmental degradation. The seminar culminates in the signing of the Tehran Declaration, which reaffirms commitments made at the Millennium World Peace Summit.
Oxford Declaration on Global Warming, July 2002	Calling climate change "a moral, ethical, and religious issue," scientists and Christian leaders from six continents call on Christian denominations, churches, and organizations to educate about climate change, reduce church buildings' impact on climate, and lobby officials to ratify the Kyoto Protocol and to reduce emissions of greenhouse gases.

Source: See endnote 22.

Environment, so that scholars of religious traditions can be in continuing dialogue with environmental scientists and policymakers.[23]

Despite the many meaningful advances to more extensive religious/environmental collaboration, serious obstacles remain. These obstacles fall under two major categories: mutual misperceptions, and differences in worldview that produce opposing positions on sensitive issues.

Misperceptions of religion by environmentalists, and of the environmental movement by people of faith today, are manifestations of the centuries-long chasm between science and spirituality, a chasm that widened by the 20th century. Near-mystical writings like those from the 19th century of John Muir, founder of the Sierra Club, which testified to the awe-inspiring power of nature, gave way in the 20th century to more scientific analysis. And in recent decades, with the emergence of the agenda that became the sustainability movement (which included environment, women's issues, and other areas on which many religions had not been vocal), the gap between the two has at times appeared unbridgeable.

In this context, a landmark 1967 essay by historian Lynn White may have contributed to the breach, at least between environmental and religious groups in the United States. In the essay, White argues that the Judeo-Christian mandate to sub-due the Earth and to be fruitful and multiply set the philo-sophical foundation for environmentally destructive industrial development in the Christian West. The claim is controversial, and has been strongly critiqued by many religious scholars, not least because White's argument is founded on just a few lines of scripture. Still, many critics of White acknowledge that parts of the Bible may have helped create a view of nature among Jews and Christians in which the natural world exists to serve humans.[24]

Sierra Club Executive Director Carl Pope takes the critique of White in a different direction, arguing that an entire gen-eration of environmentalists was soured on religion by their skewed reading of White's essay. Pope notes that environ-mentalists have widely ignored the fact that, whatever the mer-its of White's critique, he also asserted that religion would need to be part of the solution to the growing environmental cri-sis. White even ended the essay by suggesting that St. Francis of Assisi, the Tuscan lover of nature and the poor, become the patron saint of ecologists.[25]

The incomplete reading of White's essay, Pope argues, con-vinced a generation of western environmentalists that religion is the problem, and led many environmental organizations to shun religious communities in their work. But he sees this as a great mistake: Environmentalists have "made no more pro-found error than to misunderstand the mission of religion and the churches in preserving the Creation," Pope says. "For almost thirty years, we...acted as though we could save future generations, and...unnamed...species, without the full engagement of the institutions through which we save ourselves....We rejected the churches."[26]

Although the situation is improving, uneasiness between the two groups continues today, at least in the United States. Cassandra Carmichael, Director of Faith-Based Outreach at the Center for a New American Dream, a U.S. non-governmental organization (NGO) that helps Americans consume responsibly, notes that environmentalists and religious people—both of whom she works with closely—have trouble understanding each other. "Their perspectives are often different...[they] may not have experience talking or working with [each other], which is a shame, because they often share the same values when it comes to environmental sustainability." The challenge, she says, is to work out a common language that would help the two communities to work as partners.[27]

At the same time, some negative perceptions of religion are not entirely unfounded, and these pose special challenges to religious institutions and people of faith. To the extent that religion acts as a conservative societal force, it may correctly be perceived as an obstacle to sustainability, since a sustainable world will not be built without major changes to the world's economies. Where religions neglect their prophetic potential and their calling to be critics of immoral social and environmental realities, they are likely to be distrusted by those working to change those trends. Indeed, some would argue that religions and religious people today too seldom wear the radical mantle of the prophet, in the sense of being a critic of the established order. Franciscan writer and author Richard Rohr asks, "Why is it that church people by and large mirror the larger population on almost all counts?...On the whole, we tend to be just as protective of power, prestige, and possessions as everyone else."[28]

But Rohr does not despair. He sees a long tradition of reform of religion that allows it to get back to its roots—and to the power and influence found there. Paradoxically, that charismatic power emerges from an embrace of powerlessness, of vulnerability, and of spiritual freedom (liberation from undue attachment to the material world) that are found at the core of the great religions. Thus, the very reform of religion that could benefit the effort to heal the planet and its people might also give religion new relevance.[29]

Beyond the differences in perception lie tensions that emerge from differing worldviews. Consider the issue of women's status. Advocates of sustainability often view women as being denied equality and even oppressed by some religions, while some religions see the question of gender equality as a non-starter, given their view that family and societal roles played by men and women are naturally different. Because of the central role of women in combating malnutrition, reducing infectious disease, promoting education, and stabilizing populations, the perception that religion contributes to the marginalization of half of humanity is a serious obstacle for collaboration on development issues. On the other hand, the fact that women are the most involved gender in all of the world's religions offers hope that their voices will one day carry equal weight with those of men.[30]

Similarly, divergent views of when human personhood begins—at conception, or later—have left many religious people and sustainability advocates at odds over abortion, an especially sensitive issue. Representatives of the Vatican and of Muslim countries, for example, battled with proponents of reproductive rights over language to be included in the final declaration from the International Conference on Population and Development in Cairo in 1995—a battle that left each side more wary than ever about prospects for future dialogue, much less cooperation. As long as the two communities hold their current positions, cooperation is unlikely on those issues, which doesn't mean there can't be cooperation on other issues.[31]

The profound issue of what constitutes truth is another difference in worldview that can separate the two communities. Some religious positions are based on a belief that the universe contains a set of objective truths—things that are true in all places, at all times—such as that God exists, or that all sentient beings have a right to live. For many people of faith, objective truth is not negotiable. When the two communities are separated by an issue that religious people see as containing an objective truth, compromise would seem to be impossible. Again, on such issues, the two sides may simply need to agree to disagree—or be willing to engage in a respectful dialogue in which each side is open to the possibility of a shift in position.

In addition, different perspectives on the place of humanity in the natural order can also separate the two communities—and create divisions within them. Some deep ecologists, for example, see humans as just another of many species in the natural world, with no greater or lesser moral value than other species, while more mainstream environmentalists would assign a special place to humanity, even as they demand that humans live in a way that respects the entire natural world. Similar divisions can be found among spiritually inclined people as well, with some spiritual adherents to the Gaia hypothesis—the idea that the planet is a single, interconnected organism, all of which is vital taking positions similar to those of deep ecologists.[32]

Despite the tremendous challenges, collaboration is possible, even between science-oriented environmentalists and scripture-centered religious traditions. Evangelical Christians in the United States, for example, have formed an Evangelical Environmental Network to promote conservation and environmental stewardship—not only because of scientific arguments for conservation, but because they believe the natural world is God's creation and must therefore be protected. The group is credited with playing a pivotal role in blocking attempts in the U.S. Congress in 1996 to weaken the Endangered Species Act, calling the Act the "Noah's Ark of our day" for its role in preserving species, and accusing Congress of "trying to sink it." The credibility of the evangelical group with moderate members of Congress—combined with a $1 million lobbying effort—helped persuade some of those members not to disembowel the Act.[33]

Perhaps the key to engagement of the two communities is found in the perspective of the Center for a New American Dream's Cassandra Carmichael. She stresses that collaboration between religious people and sustainability advocates does not require complete agreement on all issues. Indeed, she cites examples of groups that have worked successfully together on a single issue, despite deep disagreements on a range of other topics. By simply choosing to focus on what they *can* do together, rather than on what they cannot, the collaborators were able to move ahead on a common agenda. Conceivably, other environmentalists and religious groups, most of whom share a great deal in common even if they differ sharply on some issues, could profit from the same approach.[34]

The Environment as Sacred Ground

Long a source of societal change, religion has the potential to fundamentally affect how humans relate to the natural environment. Ritual, as previously noted, was central in regulating the use of trees, rivers, and other resources by indigenous peoples and could conceivably be adapted to other cultures. More broadly, the values that mold our perspective of nature "come primarily from religious worldviews and ethical practices," according to Mary Evelyn Tucker and John Grim of the Forum on Religion and Ecology at Harvard University's Center for the Environment. Given the power of religion to shape our views of nature, religious teachings about the natural world in this era could influence how quickly or easily the world makes the transition to sustainable economies. Growing religious interest in environmentally friendly ethics and practices suggests that the world's religions are beginning to use their many assets to advance this teaching role.[35]

Consider, for example, the many statements in recent years by religious leaders on behalf of the environment. (See Table 3.) Since the mid-1980s, the Dalai Lama has made environmental protection the theme of numerous major statements—including several speeches at the Earth Summit in 1992—and environmental protection is one of the five points of his peace plan for Tibet. Ecumenical Patriarch Bartholomew, symbolic leader of the 250-million member Orthodox Church, has been in the forefront of bringing people together to study water-related environmental issues. And Pope John Paul II issued major environmental statements in 1990 and 2001, and a joint statement with Patriarch Bartholomew in June 2002.[36]

Ecumenical Patriarch Bartholomew, in particular, has effectively leveraged moral authority and church resources for environmental and social ends. Elected by the Holy Synod in 1992, the Patriarch has made environmental awareness and ecumenical dialogue an important pursuit of his patriarchate. In addition to regular environmental statements, he established Religion, Science and the Environment (RSE) in 1994, an organization that has invited religious and political leaders, scientists, journalists, and theologians for symposia and training; in the process he has raised the profile of environmental issues in the Aegean Sea, the Black Sea, down the Danube River, and in the Adriatic Sea.[37]

Perhaps the most influential of the RSE initiatives have been the biennial shipboard symposia hosted by the Patriarch that focus on water-related environmental issues. Aboard a chartered ship for approximately one week, scientists, theologians, and journalists hear dozens of lectures on the environmental problems facing the area through which they are traveling. The participants tend to be influential: in addition to the Patriarch, the 2002 Adriatic Sea symposium included a special consultant to the U.N. Secretary-General, the former head of UNEP, the head of the U.N. Development Programme, two Roman Catholic cardinals, the Primate of the Church of Sweden, imams from Egypt and Syria, a sheikh from Albania and the grand imam of Bosnia Herzegovina, several ambassadors, several heads of environmental and development-oriented NGOs, the president of the U.N. Foundation, and some 40 journalists. Sharing meals and living quarters, lectures, and field trips, these high-profile participants and other attendees learn and network with each other, to impressive effect. The Adriatic symposium ended in Venice with the Ecumenical Patriarch and Pope John Paul II signing a joint declaration on environmental protection.[38]

The gatherings focus on bodies of water in real trouble, such as the Black Sea, now the most degraded marine area in

TABLE 3

Examples of Recent Statements on the Environment by Religious Leaders and Organizations

Leader or Organization	Statement
Indigenous: Native Homelands Climate Workshop-Summit, The Albuquerque Declaration	Our Peoples and lands are a scattering of islands within a sea of our neighbors, the richest material nations in the world. The world is beginning to recognize that today's market-driven economies are not sustainable and place in jeopardy the existence of future generations. It is upsetting the natural order and laws created for all our benefit. The continued extraction and destruction of natural resources is unsustainable.
Christian: Ecumenical Patriarch Bartholomew and Pope John Paul II	An awareness of the relationship between God and humankind brings a fuller sense of the importance of the relationship between human beings and the natural environment, which is God's creation and which God entrusted to us to guard with wisdom and love.
Buddhist: Venerable Lungrig Nomgayal Abbot	Buddhism is a religion of love, understanding, and compassion and is committed towards the ideal of non-violence. As such, it also attaches great importance towards wildlife and the protection of the environment on which every being in this world depends for survival.
Hindu: Dr. Karan Singh, President, Hindu Virat Samaj	The Hindu tradition of reverence for nature and all forms of life, vegetable or animal, represents a powerful tradition which needs to be re-nurtured and re-applied in our contemporary context.
Interfaith: National Religious Partnership for the Environment	It is what God made and beheld as good that is under assault. The future of this gift so freely given is in our hands, and we must maintain it as we have received it. This is an inescapably religious challenge. We feel a profound and urgent call to respond with all we have, all we are, and all we believe.
Catholic: Pope John Paul II, "On the Ecological Crisis"	Today, the dramatic threat of ecological breakdown is teaching us the extent to which greed and selfishness—both individual and collective—are contrary to the order of creation, an order which is characterized by mutual interdependence.
Jewish: Rabbi Arthur	The encounter of God and man in nature is... conceived in Judaism as a seamless web with man as the leader,

Table 3 (continued)

Hertzberg, Vice President, World Jewish Congress	and custodian, of the natural world.... It is our Jewish responsibility to put the defense of the whole of nature at the very center of our concern.
Muslim: Dr. Abdullah Omar Nassef, Muslim World League	Unity, trusteeship, and accountability, that is *tawheed*, *khalifa*, and *akhrah*, the three central concepts of Islam, are also the pillars of the environmental ethics of Islam.... It is these values which led Muhammad, the Prophet of Islam, to say: "The world is green and beautiful and God has appointed you his stewards over it."
Bahá'í Faith: Bahá'í Delegation to United Nations Commission	Over a century ago BahAE'u'llAEh warned, "the well-being of mankind, its peace and security, are unattainable unless and until its unity is firmly established." Only upon a foundation of genuine unity, harmony, and understanding among the diverse peoples and nations of the world can a sustainable global society be erected.
Unitarian Universalist: The Seventh Guiding Principle	We affirm and promote...respect for the interdependent web of all existence of which we are a part.

Source: See endnote 36.

Europe. Described as "catastrophic," damage to the sea in the past three decades has resulted from coastal development, invasion of exotic species, damming of rivers feeding the sea, and the growing burden of fertilizer runoff and other pollutants. The 1997 symposium visited ports in six countries, sponsored field trips to degraded areas, and offered more than 30 lectures. Beyond building relationships among scientists and religious leaders and raising public environmental awareness through the hundreds of news reports generated by participating journalists, the trip inspired concrete initiatives on behalf of the environment. It gave rise to the Halki Ecological Institute, for example, a two-week-long program in 1999 to introduce Orthodox priests, seminary students, and journalists to the environmental ills of the Black Sea. The World Bank increased funding for a Black Sea program, one of its few grant (as distinguished from loan) initiatives, largely because a World

Bank vice president was at the 1997 symposium. And a religion-based environmental education and awareness program for the Black Sea region, sponsored by UNEP and the World Council of Churches, is now being planned, again inspired by the Black Sea symposium.[39]

Similar fruits are being reaped from the 1999 symposium on the Danube River. Participants testify to the role of this gathering in creating a sense of connection among the people of the river's nine host countries, even in the face of the ongoing Yugoslav war. "Divided peoples felt united by the river," explains Philip Weller, then a WWF program director of the Danube Carpathian project and symposium participant. "The symposium helped people to feel connected to nature." This emotional connection was possible because of the great interest generated by the Ecumenical Patriarch's participation. "People are still talking about...the Patriarch's involvement, three years after the event," notes another participant. The Patriarch's leadership is a prime example of how the moral authority of religion might be focused on building a sustainable world.[40]

Thousands of miles from southern Europe is another example of religious activism, this one drawing on moral authority of Buddhist teachings, as well as ritual, as means of influence. In Thailand, "environmentalist monks" are gaining fame for their advocacy of conservation and social justice within a Buddhist framework. These monks have weighed in on behalf of mangroves and birds and against shrimp farming and dam and pipeline construction, among other issues. But their best-known activities center on preserving forested area, a critical issue in Thailand. Whereas nearly three quarters of the country was covered by forests in 1938, only 15 percent remains forested today, the result of a national development strategy built around the export of primary products. These monks have proved effective at the local level in preserving forest and other resources, even though they account for less than 2 percent of Buddhist monks in Thailand.[41]

Environmentalist monks act from multiple motivations. Many see environmental destruction as the cause of great suf-

fering for humans and animals alike and feel bound, as Buddhists, to address it. Prhaku Pitak, a leader among environmentalist monks, for example, was affected by the suffering of
hunted animals—in particular, a monkey caught in a trap—that
he witnessed as a boy. Many also see a need to raise the level
of environmental awareness of Thai society. At a more practical level, some monks view environmental activism as a way
to reinvigorate Thai Buddhism, which lost influence decades
ago when the Thai government took over temple schools and,
more recently, when materialism further eroded the importance
of spiritual values.[42]

One example of the monks' success comes from the Thai
village of Giew Muang, where in 1991 Prhaku Pitak helped to
breathe life into an ineffective local forest conservation movement. The effort focused on a forest used by 10 surrounding
villages that had been degraded and denuded by decades of
exploitation. Through slide shows, environmental education
programs, and agricultural projects, Pitak taught villagers the
importance of forest conservation, finding ways to make his
case in a Buddhist framework. He dubbed the Buddha "the first
environmentalist" because the Buddha's life was closely integrated with forests. And he stressed the interrelatedness of trees,
water supply, and food production, capitalizing on the Buddhist teaching of "dependent origination," the interdepend-
ence of all things.[43]

Perhaps Pitak's most creative integration of forest conservation with spirituality was his use of religious rituals to support the conservation efforts. Because many of the villagers were
animists as well as Buddhists, Pitak first followed their sug-
gestion to enlist a village elder in asking the village's guardian
spirit to bless the conservation effort. A shrine was built to the
spirit, and offerings were made, involving every household in
the village. Then Pitak turned to Buddhist rituals. Joined by 10
other monks and surrounded by the villagers, Pitak "ordained"
the largest tree in the forest, wrapping a saffron robe around
it and following most of the rite used in a normal ordination
ceremony. No villager actually viewed the tree as a monk, of
course, but as a result of this symbolic act, the conservation

effort was accepted by the entire village as being imbued with sacred meaning instead of being relegated to the sidelines as merely a civic activity. Tree ordination illustrates the power of ritual to infuse meaning into otherwise abstract efforts. Villagers were united in seeing the trees not just as resources, but as part of a larger ecological and mystical reality. As such, they were part of a millennia-long chain of humanity that has used ritual to help maintain sustainable resource use. (See Box 3.)[44]

Pitak's success at Giew Muang stems in part from the prestige he enjoys as a monk. Some 90 percent of Thais are Buddhists, and most hold monks in high regard. His moral authority was also useful in gaining allies for his work. Pitak knew that monks alone would not save the forests of Thailand, so he reached out to the broader society to enhance the effectiveness of his activities, inviting local government officials, journalists, and NGO workers to the ordination ceremony, in addition to his own religious superiors. The publicity and alliance-building value of this inclusive strategy helped Pitak broaden the base of support for his efforts. Pitak and other environmentalist monks now regularly collaborate with environmental NGOs.[45]

Another local case, the effort to clean up the Ganges River in India, illustrates the importance that worldviews play in setting attitudes toward the environment—and the hard work and respect needed when working with widely divergent religious and secular worldviews. The Ganges, also known as the Ganga, is one of the world's major rivers, running for more than 2,500 kilometers from the Himalayas to the Bay of Bengal. It is also one of the most polluted, primarily from sewage but also from animal carcasses, human corpses, and soap and other pollutants from bathers. Scientists measure fecal coliform levels at thousands of times above what is permissible, and levels of oxygen in the water are similarly unhealthy. Renewal efforts have centered primarily on the government-sponsored Ganga Action Plan (GAP), started in 1985 with the goal of cleaning up the river by 1993. Several western-style sewage treatment plants were built along the river, but they were poorly designed, poorly maintained, and prone to shut

BOX 3

The Link Between Ritual, Ecology, and Sustainable Cultures

For thousands of years, ritual has played a central role in governing sustainable use of the natural environment. The Tsembaga people of New Guinea, for example, use ritual to allocate scarce protein for their people in a way that does not cause irreversible damage to the land. The Tukano of the Northwest Amazon employ myth and ritual to prevent overhunting and overfishing in their territory. And in the longest continually inhabited place in the United States, the Hopi village of Oraibi, people spend up to half of their time in ritual activity during certain parts of the year. Among all enduring cultures, ritual has been "a sophisticated social and spiritual technology" that helped people to live in harmony with the natural world.

Today, some traditional societies are resurrecting abandoned rituals to revive their cultures and preserve the ecological foundations of their existence. In the 2,000-year-old Ifugao culture in the Philippines, ancient hillside rice terraces are included on UNESCO's World Heritage List of significant cultural artifacts. The Ifugao culture has eroded in recent decades due to the migration of many young people to urban areas, and as a result the terraces have been in poor repair. Since 1970, technical programs have been put into place for the physical preservation of the terraces, but little was done to protect and fortify the culture until 2000, when the National Commission for Culture and the Arts spearheaded a revival of an ancient farming ritual called Patipat, last celebrated in 1944.

Village men dress in traditional red loincloths and adorn themselves with the crimson leaves of the Ti plant, which are used in special rituals. They beat on wooden shields known as tagtags as they dance through the village. Joined by dancers, including children, from the neighboring village, the groups make their way down the terraces, raising a ruckus by whooping and beating their tagtags. The ritual has both a religious and an ecological purpose: the deafening noise is meant to drive away evil spirits as well as rats. The rats are serious pests—not only because they eat crops, but because they burrow, leaving tunnels that cause seepage and erosion. The dancers continue downward, terrace by terrace, until the spirits and the rats are driven away.

Source: See endnote 44.

down during the region's frequent power outages. The GAP has been a colossal failure, and many argue that the river is more polluted now than it was in 1985.[46]

There is another view of the river, however, that parallels the scientific one. Hindus revere the Ganga as a goddess, a sacred river whose waters are, by definition, pure. Believers flock to it to bathe, in the conviction that the river's water will cleanse them, even removing their sins. Indeed, along the seven-kilometer stretch at Varanasi, one of India's most sacred cities, some 60,000 pilgrims take a "holy dip" each day. In addition, many Hindus long to have their cremated remains disposed of in the Ganga in order to release them from the ongoing cycle of suffering that governs life in the material world. To Hindus, the river is much more than a conduit for Himalayan snowmelt. It is also more than the lifeline for a 3,000-year-old civilization. It is Mother Ganga, the source of eternal life.[47]

The divergent Hindu view of the river is complemented by an equally divergent perspective on the cause of the river's abuse. Many Hindu priests see Ganga pollution not as the product of a faulty sewage policy but as a consequence of moral decay. In the Hindu cosmology of cyclical history, the current era is the Kali Yuga, the recurring epoch in which degeneracy runs rampant. Money and power have corrupted society, say the priests, and much of the activity on the river is driven by money—from industrial plants that abuse the river to the government sewage plants that have failed to clean it up.[48]

The difference in Hindu and secular perspectives on the river could not be more stark. As one researcher put it, whereas scientists, government, and NGOs measure how polluted the Ganga has become, religious people ponder "how Ganga herself might help reset the degenerate moral and cosmic order." Indeed, to many Hindus it is a grave insult to describe Mother Ganga as polluted. They do not deny that foul material has been dumped in the river, nor do they dispute the scientific reality of high levels of fecal coliform. But for many Hindus, these are mundane issues with no relevance to the Ganga's spiritual essence. Indeed, Mother Ganga's essential purity leaves some Hindus unmoved by the calls for a cleanup, since it would make no difference to Mother Ganga's essential identity. Others, however, see cleanup as a way of respecting and honoring Mother Ganga. In any case, these sensitivities complicate religious involvement in ending abuse of the Ganga.[49]

Yet such engagement is possible, as evidenced by the activities of Dr. V. B. Mishra, a hydrologist and professor of civil engineering who has been working for more than two decades to rid the river of contaminants. He is also the mahant, or head priest, of the Sankat Mochan Temple in Varanasi. With his two professional hats, Mishra embodies the two worldviews, and he finds both necessary for a complete understanding of the river. "Science and technology are one bank of the river," he explains, "and faith is the other....Both are needed to contain the river and ensure its survival." With only one bank, he says, the river would spill away and disappear.[50]

Mishra has brought his integrated perspective to his activism, although he is careful about which hat is given greater prominence at any particular moment. In 1984, he founded the secular Sankat Mochan Foundation to launch a Clean Ganga Campaign, intended to rid the river of its contaminants. From the beginning, the group had religious adherents, perhaps attracted by the comfort of working with a man who, like themselves, took a holy dip in the river each day. The efforts of his group prompted the government to launch the GAP in 1985. (The foundation later opposed the government efforts, however, because they used capital-intensive western technologies that proved inadequate for India.) More recently, the foundation has worked to bring alternative sewage technology to the river—technology that will be more reliable than the high-tech but fragile projects built by the GAP.[51]

Today, the Clean Ganga Campaign is careful to respect the distinction between physical cleanness and spiritual purity in its campaign for the Ganga. It maintains respect for religious belief in Ganga's purification power even as it promotes measures to reduce the material waste load on the river. By carefully making the distinction between cleanness and purity, the campaign earns the respect of both sides, and helps to create a collaboration between Hinduism and science.[52]

Ethical Consumption

Religions have long had a strong interest in restraining consumption, although for reasons very different from the concerns of environmentalists. The ecological argument against excessive consumption—that population growth, ever-greater levels of individual consumption, and one-time use of materials have combined to deplete stocks of raw materials and to degrade ecosystems—is well established and stands on its own. But religious traditions broaden the discussion by citing the corrosive effect of excessive consumption not only on the environment, but on the development of character, both of individuals and of societies. (See Table 4.) Living simply, many religions teach, frees up resources for those in need, and frees the human spirit to cultivate relationships with neighbors, with the natural world, and with the world of spirit. Adding these social and spiritual arguments for moderation to the newer ecological one yields a powerful case for simplicity, and situates consumption more clearly in a comprehensive understanding of what it means to be a developed person and a developed society.[53]

Despite a legacy of teachings on the spiritual corruption associated with excessive attachment to wealth or material accumulation, religious leaders and institutions in industrial nations have largely failed to reverse the consumerist engine that drives industrial economies, occasional statements on the topic notwithstanding. Concrete initiatives to promote simple living—such as simplicity circles in pockets of the United States and Europe, where neighbors gather to discuss how to achieve simplicity in a high-consumption culture—are few, and most are not promoted or sponsored by organized religion. The newly installed Archbishop of Canterbury, Rowan Williams, has said that curbing the culture of consumption will be a major focus of his ministry as head of the Anglican Church. But he must be sobered by the experience of Pope John Paul II, who set as a strategic goal of his papacy a dampening of the influence of consumerism in industrial cultures. Despite centuries of experience preaching against the illusion of satisfaction provided by earthly wealth, religion in industrial countries is struggling in its efforts to counter the consumerist tide.[54]

These traditions might find encouragement in the spiritually rooted ethic of moderate consumption found in a developing country, Sri Lanka. Since 1958, a grassroots development effort there known as Sarvodaya Shramadana has promoted village-based development programs that explicitly integrate material and spiritual development. The movement, whose name roughly means "awakening of all through sharing," motivates villagers to undertake a broad range of development projects, from latrine building to establishment of preschools and cultural centers, within a framework of Buddhist principles. The movement has grown to encompass more than half of the country's 24,000 villages and is now the largest development NGO in Sri Lanka. Its success draws on two major assets that religion brings to development: the motivational power of religious principles and the capacity to generate and use "social capital" for development.[55]

Buddhist principles are central to Sarvodaya's vision of development, and from this vision emerges the Sarvodayan ethic of consumption. In the Buddhist worldview, the goal in life is spiritual awakening, or enlightenment, which requires a person to overcome desire—the source of all human suffering, according to the Buddha. Overcoming desire, in turn, requires a spiritual detachment from material goods, so that one is indifferent to them, neither craving goods nor rejecting them. This posture of indifference is difficult to achieve in a culture of mass consumption, where advertisers conflate needs and desires and promote acquisitiveness. Thus, for Sarvodayans, consumption is not an end in itself, as it often is in the West, where consumption is regarded as a prime engine of economic growth. Instead, Sarvodayans see consumption as a tool: it provides the material platform needed to support the spiritual work of arriving at enlightenment.[56]

Indeed, one of the distinguishing features of the Sarvodayan vision of development is that it explicitly and deliberately includes not just the material requisites for a dignified life,

but also the educational, social, cultural, and spiritual requirements. This broad perspective is reflected in the list of 10
major human needs that guide Sarvodayan development work:
  • a clean and beautiful environment,
  • a clean and adequate supply of water,
  • basic clothing,
  • a balanced diet,
  • a simple house to live in,
  • basic health care,
  • simple communications facilities,
  • basic energy requirements,
  • well-rounded education, and
  • cultural and spiritual sustenance.[57]

The list of 10 basic needs is consistent with this consumption ethic. By placing nonmaterial needs on a par with
material ones, it reminds Sarvodayans of the importance of spiritual needs and of how they can be subverted by attachment
to material goods. The list also implicitly suggests where to draw
the line on consumption. If meeting the 10 needs essentially
provides for a decent life, all other desires would seem to be
expressions of "greed, sloth, or ignorance," in the words of one
Sarvodaya observer, and would not further a person's development. Thus the list produces a materially narrower but spiritually broader understanding of development than the one
prevailing in societies of mass consumption.[58]

Also underlying the Sarvodayan vision of development is
a principle of social justice that is important in shaping a consumption ethic. Dr. A. Ariyaratne, founder of the movement,
notes that one purpose of the list of 10 basic needs is to analyze
the development status of the weakest group in the community,
then work to improve its position. By limiting the list to real
needs, this recalibration function is far more feasible than if the
list essentially embraced a wide range of human desires. Indeed,
the Sarvodaya goal is a "no poverty, no affluence" society.[59]

In a more subtle but still powerful way, the social capital created by Sarvodaya activities seems to reinforce an ethic
of moderate consumption. The word *shramadana* refers to the
voluntary gift of labor made by villagers in Sarvodaya projects,

TABLE 4

Religious Teachings on Consumption

Religion or Faith	Quotation
Indigenous: Micmac Chief, North America	Miserable as we seem in thy eyes, we consider ourselves... much happier than thou, in this that we are very content with the little that we have.
Judaism: Isaiah 55:2	Why do you spend your money for that which is not broad, and your labor for that which does not satisfy?
Christianity: 1 John 3.17	How does God's love abide in anyone who has the world's goods and sees a brother or sister in need and yet refuses to help?
Islam: Qu'ran 7.31	Eat and drink, but waste not by excess; verily He loves not the excessive.
Taoism: Tao Te Ching, Chapter 33	He who knows he has enough is rich.
Hinduism: Acarangasutra 2.114-19	On gaining the desired object, one should not feel elated. On not receiving the desired object, one should not feel dejected. In case of obtaining anything in excess, one should not hoard it. One should abstain from acquisitiveness.
Confucianism: Confucius, XI.15	Excess and deficiency are equally at fault.
Buddhism: Buddhadasa Bhikkhu	The deep sense of calm that nature provides...protects our heart and mind. The lessons nature teaches us lead to a new birth beyond suffering caused by our acquisitive self-preoccupation.
Bahá'í Faith: The Bahá'í Statement on Nature	The major threats to our world environment...are manifestations of a world-encompassing sickness of the human spirit, a sickness that is marked by an overemphasis on material things and a self-centeredness that inhibits our ability to work together as a global community.

Source: See endnote 53.

such as road building, clearing an irrigation ditch, or other activities that benefit the village as a whole. Sharing pervades the movement's philosophy—as part of their work project, villagers eat together, sharing food that each has contributed. They include chants, prayers, and meditation as part of the project. They share ideas. And they share a commitment to what Buddhists know as "right speech"—encouragement, praise, and the avoidance of gossip and slander.[60]

The emphasis on sharing creates strong community ties; in fact, studies identify increased cohesion and village unity as one of the most important outcomes of the work camps. This social outcome may in fact be more important than the physical achievements of the project, because it fosters long-lasting ties of mutual trust and communication that make other community initiatives possible. In one village, for example, the practice of sharing food during the work camp prompted villagers to institute a monthly potluck meal after the project ended.[61]

While Sarvodaya is inspiring adherents to moderate consumption, western religions are showing signs of flexing their market muscle to steer consumption in a greener direction. Such activities are an adaptation of the established religious practice of using boycotts to influence corporations on issues of social justice. Religious support globally for the boycott of Nestlé products in the 1970s, for example, pressured that company to end its aggressive marketing of baby formula in developing countries, where it had too often displaced breast-feeding, the healthier approach. And churches were strong backers of grape and lettuce boycotts in support of the United Farm Workers in California in the 1960s and 1970s.[62]

Today some congregations are moving beyond boycotts to help steer consumption toward green companies, largely by harnessing another great religious asset—the sheer mass of adherents—toward green consumption. Because of the substantial market presence of people of faith, these fledgling efforts could potentially have a large impact. One creative example in the United States is the work of the Regeneration Project in California, an initiative of the Episcopal Church. It includes Episcopal Power and Light (EP&L), a ministry that promotes green energy and energy efficiency. EP&L was started in 1996 when Reverend Sally Bingham realized that she might capitalize on the state's deregulation of energy to persuade a bloc of customers—the state's Episcopalians—to choose energy generated from renewable sources, such as wind, geothermal, and biomass. The project also encourages participating parishes to undertake an energy audit of their buildings. The Regeneration Project includes California Interfaith Power and Light, which does political advocacy to promote renewable energy.[63]

In its short life, the Regeneration Project has spread to seven states, and it could have a substantial effect on energy consumption patterns if adopted by religious groups and adherents nationwide. In addition to offering a shot in the arm for emerging renewable energy companies, the project could help boost energy conservation. A 1995 U.S. Environmental Protection Agency (EPA) survey of commercial buildings calculated that an energy efficiency upgrade of the country's 269,000 houses of worship—which account for about 5 percent of US commercial building floor space—would prevent 6 million tons of carbon dioxide from being released to the atmosphere, while saving congregations more than $500 million.[64]

The carbon savings would be only a tiny fraction of U.S. carbon emissions, but the real returns would come from enlisting congregant support for similar conservation activities in their homes. Of the 12 categories of commercial buildings designated by the U.S. Department of Energy and used in the EPA survey, only office buildings are visited by more adults more frequently than houses of worship. Indeed, the 44 percent of the American public who regularly visit a church, synagogue, or mosque constitutes a huge pool of potential converts to energy efficiency and green energy sources, especially if efforts to green the church are accompanied by efforts to raise consciousness among congregants, as in the EP&L program.[65]

Another effort to practice ethical consumption is religious participation in the Interfaith Coffee Program run by Equal Exchange, a for-profit U.S. company. The company sells only coffee that is "fair-traded," which means that participating farmers are guaranteed a minimum price for their harvest, no matter what market conditions might dictate. This helps farmers avoid the erratic price swings that characterize many international commodity markets and gives them greater economic stability. Equal Exchange is also committed to helping farmers secure credit at rates they can afford and to encouraging ecologically sustainable farming practices, including organic and shade-grown cultivation.[66]

Equal Exchange recognized that its ethical approach to coffee might appeal to people of faith. They knew, too, that many Americans are regular churchgoers, and that some of them attend "coffee hours" after services. So they established the Interfaith Coffee Program to encourage congregations and individuals to switch to fair-traded coffee. Begun in 1997 as a partnership with the aid agency Lutheran World Relief, the program now includes the American Friends Service Committee, the Presbyterian Church USA, and the Unitarian Universalist Service Committee. While small, it has grown rapidly: more than 3,500 congregations participated at the end of 2001, just over 1 percent of all the houses of worship in the United States, but up from a handful when the program started. The Interfaith program is the fastest-growing segment of Equal Exchange's business, and now accounts for 11 percent of the firm's sales.[67]

As with green energy, the potential for people of faith to change coffee consumption patterns is huge. Coffee is the second most widely consumed beverage in the United States, and its ethical consumption requires little or no sacrifice. Yet drinking fair-traded coffee yields great personal satisfaction—it's "drinking a cup of justice," in the words of one Lutheran Interfaith Coffee participant. With 99 percent of the institutional religious market untouched, the program would have a major impact on the U.S. coffee market if religious groups nationwide were to climb on board—and if participating congregants were persuaded to take their new habit home.[68]

The coffee program offers extensive opportunities to educate congregations about a host of justice issues, from the terms of trade in international commerce to the value of co-ops and organic farming. It can help people of faith, who have long supported aid and relief programs, to broaden their efforts beyond charity and into justice. Grasping this bigger picture, one participant noted that "our consumer dollars are hurting the very people our offering dollars are trying to help." Such

consciousness-raising can spark a "virtuous circle," as con-
sumers begin to consider the effects of other patterns of consumption on far-flung people and places.[69]

Another potentially high-leverage area for introducing
ethics into economic decisions is through financial investments.
As noted, religious institutions are already active in holding corporations accountable for their practices through the use of
shareholder resolutions. This consciousness, extended to religious individuals, could have a substantial effect on investment
patterns. Socially responsible investment (SRI) accounted for
only 12 percent of all investments in 2000. Religiously led cam-
paigns to persuade the 44 percent of Americans who attend religious services at least monthly to shift their investment dollars
to SRI could give a substantial boost to the SRI movement.[70]

Accelerating Engagement

In pockets of activity worldwide, many religions are beginning to show interest in building a sustainable world, as the
record of the past decade demonstrates. At the same time, advocates of sustainability are becoming somewhat more receptive
to spiritual appeals, as seen in the World Wildlife Fund collaboration with churches along the Danube River, or the ad initiative by the National Council of Churches and the Sierra Club
in the United States. More extensive engagement of environmentalism by the religious community, and of spirituality by
the environmental and development communities is needed
and is in the interest of both. Some of this engagement can
occur in the form of partnerships. Some can take place within
each community. If the conditions are indeed ripe to build
bridges between the two groups, such initiatives could conceivably contribute to a historic ending to the schism between
science and spirit.

At the international level, several organizations have
shown leadership in bringing about this engagement, setting
an example for the work of local religious and environmental

communities. UNEP, for example, has published resources on faiths and the environment dating back to 1991. It has given guidance and support to the Interfaith Partnership for the Environment, a group of scholars from diverse faiths, in various projects, among them the publication of a book describing the posture of major religions toward the environment. Under considerable criticism, the World Bank has held major interfaith meetings on development questions since 1998, out of which emerged the World Faiths Development Dialogue (WFDD), which has increased religious input to the work of the Bank. On the religious side, the World Council of Churches' Climate Change Programme was formed in 1988 to lobby governments and international organizations to work for policies to combat climate change.[71]

To move the work of engagement forward, it is important to make use of the valuable assets that each side brings to the table. Religions could use their asset base—their ability to shape worldviews, their authority, numbers, material resources, and capacity to build community—to advance the work of sustainability. Each religious tradition will know how to best use its particular strengths; the mix of actions will vary from tradition to tradition and from place to place. For each of the five asset areas, any number of activities is possible. (See Table 5.)

In the arena of moral authority—perhaps the most powerful asset religions possess—several initiatives are possible. First, religious leaders might use their elevated social standing to call for an end to systematic abuse of the environment and for the creation of a just and environmentally healthy world in a way that would capture the attention of many people.

Efforts such as the WWF-sponsored meeting of religious leaders in Assisi in 1986 or the Ecumenical Patriarch's symposia for religious leaders and scientists are good models of the ecumenical spirit needed to expand the openness of each community to the perspective of the other.

Imagine stepping up a few notches the bold initiative of the Ecumenical Patriarch in co-signing an environmental declaration with the Pope. Suppose that these western religious leaders, along with the Dalai Lama, the Grand Muftis of Syria, and leaders of a dozen other religions, were to travel to the North Pole to bear witness to a melting world, and to call for action to stop it. Or suppose they were to hold an inter-religious prayer vigil outside the annual meetings of the World Bank, calling attention to policies that serve to increase the miseries of the poor. Such leadership would lift discussion of these issues to an entirely new level, and might well increase pressure for action. It might also enhance the prestige of religion, as followers and critics alike would gain new respect for leaders who demonstrated a willingness to grapple seriously with difficult contemporary challenges.

Wrestling with contemporary challenges could help religions augment their moral authority in another way. If they read the "signs of the times" through the lens of their own scriptures, religious traditions might demonstrate the relevance of their teachings for the major issues of our day, by helping to address the tremendous environmental and social needs of this moment in history. Several tools—known as retrieval, re-evaluation, and reconstruction—are used by some theologians for evaluating scripture and tradition in the light of contemporary circumstances.[72]

In the first instance, many religions retrieve teachings that have lain dormant but that are especially relevant today. One example of this was the revival in the last decade of the Hebrew tradition of the Jubilee—the teaching from Leviticus that debts should be forgiven, and slaves freed, every 50 years—to generate support for the goal of reducing the debt of the world's poorest nations. Known for millennia, this scriptural teaching became particularly evocative in the 1990s because of contemporary circumstances. Poor countries were struggling under the burden of huge debt payments, which were siphoning off the money available for investments in health and education. As the year 2000 approached, and nations searched for a meaningful way to mark the millennium, the Jubilee tradition spoke to the global community in a new and fresh way.[73]

Arguably the most powerful latent teaching in many faith traditions is the exhortation to avoid preoccupation

TABLE 5

Leveraging Religious Assets

Asset	Approaches to Consider
Worldview development	• Assess teachings; ensure that the natural world is sufficiently represented in worldview and ethics.
Moral authority	• Use the pulpit to address the global crisis of sustainability. • Use the congregational newsletter, bulletin, or Web site as a platform. • Make effective use of the media, through placement of op-eds, letters to the editor, and coverage of congregation's environmental activities. • Engage political leaders who make decisions affecting sustainability.
Members	• Encourage members to write letters, join boycotts or protests, or in other ways creatively bring their full political weight to bear on these issues. • Educate members about consumption and encourage them to consume less and to buy products that have low environmental impact. • Encourage members to shift investments to companies with exemplary environmental and labor records.
Material resources	• Use physical facilities as a venue for discussing issues of sustainability, or for organizing sustainability activities. • Use physical facilities as a showcase of simplicity, and for renewable energy, energy conservation, organic gardening, or other activities that could promote sustainable living. • Shift purchasing and investment decisions to favor a sustainable world.
Community building	• Increase bonds of trust and communication, and deepen emotional ties to the environment, by organizing environmentally oriented service activities. • Build on existing social ties to support congregants in attempts to simplify their lives.

Source: Worldwatch Institute.

with wealth and materialism. Excessive consumption is the engine that runs the world's most powerful economies, and the arguments used to resist it—it is bad for the environment, and often bad for human health—have made only small dents in the trend. Religions are in a position to weigh in more strongly with the spiritual and moral case against excessive consumption: that it diverts attention from the most important goals of life, and that it squanders resources that might be used to help the poor. And beyond preaching, they could become more active in the community by sponsoring neighborhood groups that seek to promote simplicity and by otherwise offering support to those who seek to live simply.

Religions also reevaluate and reconstruct traditional teachings in light of present realities. A good example of this comes from Africa, where the high rates of HIV infection have pushed some churches and mosques to rethink their teachings on condom use. Increasingly uncomfortable with prohibition of condom use as they watch masses of people—often their own congregants—lie sick and dying from a disease that prophylactics could largely prevent, many local leaders have questioned the policy. Muslim communities in several African nations have changed direction on teachings about condoms. And a Catholic bishop in South Africa has called for a reversal of his church's teaching on condom use.[74]

Whether these particular re-evaluations and reconstructions should be adopted broadly by various religions is a question to be decided by each tradition. The point here is simply that established religions have centuries of experience reading their central tenets in the light of contemporary realities. Indeed, it is the adaptability of religion, which results from the universality and timelessness of core teachings, that helps to make it one of the most enduring of human institutions. Some scholars even suggest replacing the term "religious traditions" with "religious processes," so consistent is the theme of adaptation in the history of most religions.[75]

The challenge for environmentalists and other advocates of sustainability, meanwhile, may be to build a greater appreciation for the importance of spirituality into their own work. Public overtures toward people's spiritual sensibilities could be a powerful step forward for sustainability. This is important not simply to win religious people as allies, but because spirituality is important for development. All development activities are embedded in a cultural context; if pursued unwisely, they can provoke a cultural backlash. The Shah of Iran, in his attempt to "modernize" that country between the 1950s and 1970s, paid too little attention to religious sensibilities in the process and learned firsthand, through the 1979 revolution that dethroned him, how costly this insensitivity can be.

A good demonstration of the sensitivity needed is found at the United Nations Population Fund (UNFPA), which works around the world on issues of reproductive health. In Kenya, where UNFPA seeks to prevent the spread of AIDS by halting the contraction of HIV among sex workers, the agency collaborates both with Catholic parishes and with secular health clinics—but in different ways. UNFPA underwrites the provision of condoms at the health clinic. But at the parishes, the agency follows a policy sensitive to Catholic teaching about condom use and funds programs that offer income-generating projects as an alternative to the sex work. In sum, UNFPA identifies common ground for collaboration rather than focusing on areas of difference—a helpful model for traversing the bumpy spots in the relationship between sustainability groups and some religious communities.[76]

In addition to respecting the religious sensibilities of a culture, environmentalists might seek ways to express spirituality in their own programs and communication efforts. Such expressions need not be religious, of course, but might instead focus on creating an emotional connection between the public and the natural environment—an indispensable and largely missing link in the effort to generate commitment to sustainability. As the late Harvard biologist Stephen Jay Gould suggested, "We cannot win this battle to save species and environments without forging an emotional/spritual bond between ourselves and nature as well—for we will not fight to save what we do not love."[77]

Building on Gould's thought, environmental educator David Orr challenges scientists (including environmentalists) to knead emotion into their work. He notes that most biologists and ecologists "believe that cold rationality, fearless objectivity, and a bit of technology" will get humanity out of its environmental predicament. But those tools have long been used, with minimal success. What is missing, Orr unabashedly asserts, is love. "Why is it so hard to talk about love, the most powerful of human emotions, in relation to science, the most powerful and far-reaching of human activities?" Orr asks. He notes that passion and good science, far from being antithetical, are as interdependent as the heart and the brain. Both are needed if we are to fully understand our world and our role in it.[78]

Environmentalists can help to infuse a sense of emotion into their work—to navigate using both banks of the river—by getting back to the movement's own roots. Although rare today, passionate environmental writing was once the norm for conservationists. Consider this from the writings of John Muir, founder of the Sierra Club: "Perched like a fly on this Yosemite dome, I gaze and sketch and bask...humbly prostrate before the vast display of God's power, and eager to offer self-denial and renunciation with eternal toil to learn any lesson in the divine manuscript." Such prose reaches people in a different place than the one that takes in analysis and statistics—the necessary yet limited language of modern environmentalism—and it motivates in a way that science alone cannot.[79]

By combining their considerable skills and complementary perspectives, environmentalists and religious people can help reunite our civilization's head and heart, re-engaging religion in the quest for a new cosmology, a new worldview for our time. Cultural historian Thomas Berry calls this emerging perspective a New Story —the story of a people in an intimate and caring relationship with their planet, with their cosmos, and with each other. Its ethics would deal not just with homicide and suicide, but equally with geocide and biocide (the abuse of our planet and its many life forms). It would be as comfortable with awe and wonder as with weights and measures. It would rewrite the story of unrestrained science and technology, of a human species alienated from its own home. It would be the lodestar that guides us to a socially just and environmentally sustainable future.[80]

Notes

1.   National Council of Churches website, <www.webofcreation.org/ncc/anwr.html>, viewed 17 October 2002.

2.   Common interests from Mary Evelyn Tucker, "Worldly Wonder: Religions Enter Their Ecological Phase," (Chicago: Open Court Press, forthcoming). She formulates the common interests this way: fostering reverence for the Earth, respect for other species, responsibility to the welfare of future generations, restraint in the consumption of resources, and more equitable redistribution of goods. Pakistan from IUCN–The World Conservation Union, *The Pakistan National Conservation Strategy* (Karachi, Pakistan: 1991); Orthodox from Religion, Science and the Environment (RSE) website, <www.rsesymposia.org>, and from Maria Becket, RSE Symposium coordinator, e-mail to author, 15 October 2002.

3.   Is and ought stories from Richard Norgaard, "Can Science and Religion Better Save Nature Together?" *BioScience*, September 2002, p. 842; most violent from Michael Renner, "Ending Violent Conflict," in Lester R. Brown et al., *State of the World 1999* (New York: W.W. Norton & Company, 1999); greatest environmental degradation is evident in global statistics on species extinctions, deforestation, erosion, air and water pollution, and a host of other maladies, all of which accelerated dramatically in the twentieth century. Box 1 based on Mary Evelyn Tucker and John Grim, "Introduction: The Emerging Alliance of World Religions and Ecology," in *Daedalus*, fall 2001, p. 14, <environment.harvard.edu/religion/publications/journals/ index.html>.

4.   David Loy, "The Religion of the Market," in Harold Coward and Daniel Maguire, *Visions of a New Earth: Religious Perspectives on Population, Consumption, and Ecology* (Albany: State University of New York Press, 2000), pp. 15–28.

5.   Gary Gardner and Brian Halweil, *Underfed and Overfed: The Global Epidemic of Malnutrition*, Worldwatch Paper 150 (Washington, DC: Worldwatch Institute, 1999).

6.   Religion as central to culture from Clifford Geertz, "Religion as a Cultural System," in Clifford Geertz, *Interpretation of Cultures* (New York: Basic Books, 1973), pp. 87–125.

7.   Societal drivers from Thomas Berry, *The Great Work: Our Way to the Future* (New York: Bell Tower, 1999); individual drivers from Gerald T. Gardner and Paul C. Stern, *Environmental Problems and Human Behavior* (Boston: Allyn and Bacon, 1996), pp. 21–32; Nestlé from Robin Broad and John Cavanagh, "The Corporate Accountability Movement: Lessons and Opportunities," A Study for the World Wildlife Fund's (WWF) Project on International Financial Flows and the Environment, 1998, pp. 12 and 30.

8. Mary Clark, *Ariadne's Thread* (New York: St. Martin's Press, 1989), pp. 184–85; see also Robin W. Lovin and Frank E. Reynolds, eds., *Cosmogony and Ethical Order* (Chicago: University of Chicago Press, 1985).

9. Box 2 from Mary Evelyn Tucker and John Grim, "Series Foreword," in Christopher Key Chapple and Mary Evelyn Tucker, *Hinduism and Ecology* (Cambridge, MA: Harvard University Press, 2000), pp. xxv–xxvii.

10. Mathieu Deflem, "Ritual, Anti-Structure, and Religion: A Discussion of Victor Turner's Processual Symbolic Analysis," *Journal for the Scientific Study of Religion*, vol. 30, no. 1 (1991), pp. 1–25; Robert Bellah, "Civil Religion in America," *Daedalus* 96 (1967), pp. 1–21.

11. Ritual and resource management from E.N. Anderson, *Ecologies of the Heart: Emotion, Belief, and the Environment* (New York: Oxford University Press, 1996), p. 166; ritual and emotional connections from Anderson, op. cit. this note, p. 166.

12. Stalin quoted in Winston Churchill, *The Second World War: The Gathering Storm* (Boston: Houghton-Mifflin, 1948), p. 601; Pope and Poland from Carl Bernstein and Marco Politi, *His Holiness: John Paul II and the History of Our Time* (New York: Penguin Books, 1996), pp. 11–12; Tibet from "UN Rights Chief Pressures China on Detained Boy Panchen Lama," *Agence France Presse*, posted on web site of the Tibetan Government in Exile, <www.tibet.com/NewsRoom/panchen1.htm>, viewed 24 October 2002.

13. David Barrett and Todd Johnson, *World Christian Trends, AD 30–AD 2200* (Pasadena, CA: William Carey Library, 2001); Table 1 from ibid., and from Mary Evelyn Tucker and John Grim, professors of religion, Bucknell University, discussion with author, 19 October 2002 ("indigenous" is the category that Barrett and Johnson call "animists and shamanists").

14. Religious adherence statistics from <www.adherents.com>, viewed 24 October 2002; Pakistan from IUCN, op. cit. note 2, and from IUCN, *Final Report, Mid-Term Review of National Conservation Strategy: Mass Awareness Initiatives* (Islamabad: 2000).

15. John A. Grim, ed., *Indigenous Traditions and Ecology* (Cambridge, MA: Harvard University Press, 2001).

16. Belden, Russonello & Stewart, Research and Communications, "Americans and Biodiversity: New Perspectives in 2002," report to the Biodiversity Project, Washington, DC, February 2002, p. 3. The most common response, "to preserve the environment for our children," was mentioned by 58 percent of respondents.

17. Land area from Alliance of Religions and Conservation (ARC), at <www.religionsandconservation.org>, viewed 21 October 2002; mosques from IUCN, *Final Report*, op. cit. note 14; U.S. religious buildings is a Worldwatch estimate based on data in U.S. Department of Energy (DOE), Energy Information Administration, *1999 Commercial Buildings Energy Consumption Survey: Consumption and Expenditures Tables* (Washington, DC: 2002); schools from ARC, op. cit. this note, and from John Smith, ARC, discussion with Erik Assadourian, Worldwatch Institute, 21 October 2002; Confucian and Vedic health systems from *Financial Times*, 30 April 2002; Catholic health systems from Catholic Charities USA, <www.catholiccharitiesusa.org/Programs/Advo cacy/letters/Letters2001/sabuse1.htm>, viewed 23 April 2002.

18. Interfaith Center for Corporate Responsibility from Meg Voorhes, e-mail to author, 28 May 2002; Tracey Rembert, Shareholder Action Network, discussion with author, 15 May 2002.

19. Ismail Serageldin and Christian Grootaert, "Defining Social Capital: An Integrating View," in Partha Dagupta and Ismail Serageldin, eds., *Social Capital: A Multi-faceted Perspective* (Washington, DC: World Bank, 2000).

20. Clark, op. cit. note 8, p. 184.

21. Andrew Greeley, "Coleman Revisited: Religious Structures as a Source of Social Capital," *American Behavioral Scientist*, March/April 1997, p. 591.

22. Table 2 from the following: WWF from <www.religionsandconservation.org>; Global Forum from *Preserving and Cherishing the Earth: An Appeal for Joint Commitment in Science and Religion* (Moscow: 1990), <clawww.lmu .edu/~lvanwensveen/courses/thst398/topic7.htm>; Parliament from <www.changemakers.net/journal/02february/religionecology.cfm>; World Council of Churches, "Ecumenical Earth," <www.wcc-coe.org/wcc/ what/jpc/ecology.html>, viewed 18 October 2002; Windsor Summit from "Religions Vow a New Alliance for Conservation," *One Country*, April–June 1995; Harvard from <www.hds.harvard.edu/cswr/ecology>, viewed 21 October 2002, and from <environment.harvard.edu/religion>, viewed 21 October 2002; symposia from <www.rsesymposia.org>; Millennium Summit from <www.millenniumpeacesummit.com>; Sacred Gifts and Tehran seminar from "Religions Pledge Sacred Gifts for a Living Planet," press release (London: WWF-UK, 15 November 2000).

23. Conferences from <www.hds.harvard.edu/cswr/ecology>, viewed 21 October 2002; Forum from <environment.harvard.edu/religion>, viewed 21 October 2002. The Harvard book series and the comprehensive web site of the Forum on Religion and Ecology are helping to establish a new academic field in religion and ecology with implications for environmental policy. The web site contains introductory essays, annotated bibliographies, syllabi, video lists, statements of religious leaders, and denominations.

24. Lynn White, "The Historical Roots of Our Ecological Crisis," in Roger S. Gottlieb, *This Sacred Earth: Religion, Nature, Environment* (New York: Routledge, 1996), pp. 184–93; critique of White from J. Baird Callicott, "Genesis and John Muir," *ReVision*, 12 (winter 1990), pp. 31–46.

25. Carl Pope, "Remarks of Carl Pope, Sierra Club Executive Director, Symposium on Religion, Science and the Environment under the Auspices of His All Holiness Bartholomew I, Ecumenical Patriarch, Santa Barbara, California, November 6–8, 1997," *Ecozoic*, <www.Ecozoic.com/eco/CarlPope.asp>, viewed 9 October 2002; St. Francis from White, op. cit. note 24, pp. 192–93.

26. Pope, op. cit. note 25.

27. Cassandra Carmichael, Director of Faith-Based Outreach, Center for a New American Dream, Takoma Park, Maryland, conversation with author, 9 October 2002, and e-mail to author, 24 October 2002.

28. Richard Rohr, "We Need Transformation, Not False Transcendence," *National Catholic Reporter*, 15 February 2002.

29. Ibid.

30. Women as most involved from John Grim, Professor of Religion, Bucknell University, discussion with author, 19 October 2002.

31. Religion Counts, *Religion and Public Policy at the UN* (Washington, DC: April 2002).

32. Gaia from Anne Primavesi, *Sacred Gaia* (London: Routledge, 2000); Tibet from the Dalai Lama, "Five Point Peace Plan for Tibet," <www.tibet.net/eng/diir/enviro/hhdl/fivepoint/index.html>, viewed 18 October 2002

33. Bruce Barcot, "For God So Loved the World," *Outside*, March 2001, <web.outsidemag.com/magazine/200103/200103christian3.html>, viewed 19 October 2002.

34. Carmichael, op. cit. note 27.

35. Ritual from Anderson, op. cit. note 11, p. 166; quote from Mary Evelyn Tucker and John Grim, "Religions of the World and Ecology: Discovering the Common Ground," <environment.harvard.edu/religion/religion/index.html>, viewed 27 October 2002.

36. Table 3 from the following: National Religious Partnership for the Environment (NRPE) from "The Joint Appeal in Religion and Science: Statement by Religious Leaders at the Summit on Environment," 3 June 1991, New York City, <environment.harvard.edu/religion/publications/statements/joint_appeal.html>, viewed 16 October 2002; Bahá'í from "World Citizenship: A Global Ethic for Sustainable Development," *Bahá'í International Community Statement Library*, <www.bic-un.bahai.org/93-0614.htm>, viewed 18 October 2002; Buddhist from UNEP, *Earth and Faith: A Book of Reflection for Action* (New York: 2000), pp. 8–9; Christian from the Ecumenical Patriarch Bartholomew and Pope John Paul II, "Joint Declaration on Articulating a Code of Environmental Ethics," <www.goarch.org/en/news/releases/articles/

release8113.asp>, viewed 17 October 2002; Catholic from Pope John Paul II, "On the Ecological Crisis," delivered 8 December 1989, <www.catholic-forum .com/saints/pope0264ia.htm>, viewed 17 October 2002; Hindu from UNEP, op. cit. this note, p. 10; indigenous from Center for a New American Dream, at <www.newdream.org/faith/indigenous.html>, viewed 10 October 2002; Jewish from UNEP, op. cit. this note, p. 11; Muslim from UNEP, op. cit. this note, pp. 11–12; Unitarian Universalist from Unitarian Universalist Association, "Principles and Purposes," <www.uua.org/aboutuua/principles.html>, viewed 17 October 2002; Tibet from the Dalai Lama, "Five Point Peace Plan for Tibet," <www.tibet.net/eng/diir/enviro/hhdl/fivepoint/index.html>, viewed 18 October 2002; "Common Declaration by Pope John Paul II and Ecumenical Patriarch Bartholomew I," <www.rsesymposia.org/symposium_iv/ Common%20Declaration.pdf.

37. RSE, op. cit. note 2.

38. Symposia from Maria Becket, RSE symposium coordinator, discussion with author, 25 September 2002; other details from RSE, op. cit. note 2.

39. Black Sea from Laurence David Mee, "The Black Sea Today," <www.rse symposia.org/symposium_ii/overview_blacksea.htm>; Halki from John Chryssavgis, "Conference Report: A Symposium on the Danube: Religion and Science in Dialogue about the Environment," *Worldviews*, vol. 4 (2000), p. 82; World Bank and UNEP from John Bennett, independent consultant working with the RSE, conversation with author, 24 October 2002.

40. Philip Weller, former Program Director, WWF, discussion with author, 20 September 2002; Patriarch's involvement from Jasmina Bachmann, International Convention for the Protection of the Danube River, discussion with author, 23 September 2002.

41. Less than 2 percent from Susan M. Darlington, "Practical Spirituality and Community Forests: Monks, Ritual, and Radical Conservatism in Thailand," in Anna L. Tsing & Paul Greenough, eds., *Imagination and Distress in Southern Environmental Projects* (Durham: Duke University Press, forthcoming).

42. Motivations from Susan M. Darlington, Hampshire College, conversation with author, 22 August 2002.

43. Darlington, op. cit. note 41.

44. Darlington, op. cit. note 41. Importance of ritual from ibid. Darlington particularly stresses the community-building aspect of the ritual. Box 3 from the following: ritual throughout history from Dolores La Chapelle, "Ritual is Essential," *In Context*, spring 1984, p. 39; Ifugao from Alfred A. Yuson, "Dancing Anew on the Stairways to Heaven," *UNESCO Courier*, <www.unesco.org/ courier/2000>, December 2000.

45. Darlington, op. cit. note 41.

46. Kelly D. Alley, *On the Banks of the Ganga: When Wastewater Meets a Sacred River* (Ann Arbor: University of Michigan Press, 2002); Alexander Stille, "The Ganges' Next Life," *The New Yorker*, June 1999, pp. 58–67.

47. Kelly D. Alley, "Idioms of Degeneracy: Assessing Ganga's Purity and Pollution," in Lance E. Nelson, ed., *Purifying the Earthly Body of God: Religion and Ecology in Hindu India* (Albany: State University of New York Press, 1998), pp. 297–330.

48. Fran Peavey, President, Friends of the Ganges (San Francisco), discussion with author, 4 September 2002; Dr. V.B. Mishra, discussion with author, 5 September 2002.

49. Alley, op. cit. note 47.

50. Stille, op. cit. note 46; Dr. V. B. Mishra, op. cit. note 48.

51. Mishra, op. cit. note 48; Alley, op. cit. note 47; Stille, op. cit. note 46.

52. Cleanness and purity from Alley, op. cit. note 47, p. 305; maintains respect from ibid., p. 320; fusion from ibid., p. 317.

53. Table 4 from Center for a New American Dream, "Quotes and Teachings of World Religions on Care of the Earth and Responsible Consumption," at <www.newdream.org/faith>, viewed 16 October 2002, except for Buddhadasa Bhikkhu, from Donald K. Swearer, "Buddhism and Ecology: Challenge and Promise," *Forum on Religion and Ecology*, <environment.harvard.edu/religion/religion/buddhism/index.html>, viewed 16 October 2002.

54. "Rowan Williams Confirmed as New Archbishop of Canterbury," *Guardian Unlimited*, at <www.guardian.co.uk/religion/Story/0,2763,761857,00.html>, viewed 21 October 2002; Pope from "Pope John Paul II Addresses Overconsumption," *Green Cross*, summer 1996.

55. Sarvodaya from <www.sarvodaya.org/>, viewed 28 October 2002; Ariyaratne, quoted in Christopher Candland, "Faith as Social Capital: Religion and Community Development in Southern Asia," in *Policy Sciences*, 33 (2000), pp. 355–74.

56. Buddhism roots from A. T. Ariyaratne, *Buddhist Economics in Practice in the Sarvodaya Shramadana Movement of Sri Lanka* (Salisbury, UK: Sarvodaya Support Group, 1999), p. 7; consumption as a tool from Ariyaratne, quoted in Candland, op. cit. note 55, p. 355, and from Joanna Macy, *Dharma and Development: Religion as Resource in the Sarvodaya Self-Help Movement* (West Hartford, CT: Kumarian Press, 1991), p. 47.

57. Development vision from Macy, op. cit. note 56, p. 46; 10 needs from D. J. Mitchell, "Sarvodaya: An Introduction to the Sarvodaya Shramadana Movement in Sri Lanka," booklet of the Sarvodaya Movement (Moratuwa, Sri Lanka: undated), p.3.

58. Macy, op. cit. note 56, pp. 27, 46.

59. Ariyaratne, op. cit. note 55, pp. 9, 37.

60. Macy, op. cit. note 56, pp. 51–63.

61. Ibid., p. 53.

62. Nestlé from Broad and Cavanagh, op. cit. note 7; lettuce boycotts from Susan Ferris and Ricardo Sandoval, *The Fight in the Fields: Cesar Chavez and the Farmworkers' Movement* (New York: Harcourt Brace, 1997).

63. Regeneration Project from <www.theregenerationproject.org>, and from Sally Bingham, e-mail to Erik Assadourian, Worldwatch Institute, 21 October 2002.

64. U.S. Environmental Protection Agency (EPA), "Energy Star for Congregations," <www.epa.gov/smallbiz/congregations.html>, viewed 23 July 2002; 5 percent from DOE, op. cit. note 17, "Energy Consumption Survey: Commercial Buildings Characteristics," <www.eia.doe.gov/emeu/cbecs/char99/intro.html>, viewed 24 October 2002; EPA calculation based on a survey of commercial buildings carried out by the DOE.

65. Share of Americans at church from National Opinion Research Center, "General Social Survey 2000," at The American Religion Data Archive, <www.thearda.com>, viewed 22 October 2002.

66. Equal Exchange, <www.equalexchange.com>, viewed 23 October 2002.

67. Participating congregations from Equal Exchange, "Building Alternatives Amid Crisis," *2001 Annual Report*, <www.equalexchange.com/downloads/Annual%20Report%202001.pdf>, viewed 23 October 2002; 1 percent of houses of worship is a Worldwatch calculation based on data from Equal Exchange, op. cit. this note, and from DOE, op. cit. note 17; percentage of sales from Equal Exchange, op. cit. this note.

68. Quote from Timothy Bernard, cited in "The Interfaith Coffee Program," Equal Exchange, <www.equalexchange.com/interfaith/pcusaproject.html>, viewed 18 July 2002; coffee drinking at U.S. Department of Agriculture, Economic Research Service, Food Consumption (Per Capita) Data System: Beverages, <www.ers.usda.gov/data/foodconsumption/datasystem.asp>, viewed 28 October 2002.

69. Tim Bernard, "Brewing Faith and Coffee," Lutheran World Relief, <www.lwr.org/coffee/coffee/newcoffee.html>, viewed 23 October 2002.

70. Share of Americans at church from National Opinion Research Center, op. cit. note 65, social investment from Social Investment Forum, *2001 Report on Socially Responsible Investing Trends in the United States*, 28 November 2001,

<www.efund.com/pdfs/sri_trends_report_2001.pdf>.

71. Interfaith Partnership for the Environment and UNEP, "Earth and Faith: A Book of Reflection for Action" (New York: UNEP, 2001); WFFD from "Second Summit between World Bank and World Religions Focuses on Projects," *One Country: The Online Newsletter of the International Bahá'í Community*, <www.onecountry.org/e113/e11310as.htm>, viewed 25 October 2002; World Council of Churches, "Ecumenical Earth," <www.wcc-coe.org/wcc/what/jpc/ecology.html>, viewed 18 October 2002.

72. Tucker and Grim, op. cit. note 3, pp. 16–17.

73. Martin Wroe, "An Irresistible Force," *Sojourners*, May-June 2000.

74. Infection rate from UNAIDS, "Epidemiological Fact Sheets on HIV/AIDS and Sexually Transmitted Infections, 2002 Update: South Africa," <www.unaids.org/hivaidsinfo/statistics/fact_sheets/pdfs/Southafrica_en.pdf>, viewed 7 August 2002; Muslim communities and Catholic bishop from Thoraya Obaid, Executive Director, United Nations Population Fund, "Building Bridges for Human Development: The Role of Culture and Religion in Promoting Universal Principles of the Programme of Action on Population and Development," address at Georgetown University, 25 April 2002.

75. Tucker, op. cit. note 2.

76. Obaid, op. cit. note 74.

77. Gould quoted in David Orr, "For the Love of Life," *Conservation Biology*, December 1992, p. 486.

78. Ibid., pp. 486–87.

79. John Muir quoted in Trebbe Johnson, "The Second Creation," *Sierra Magazine*, December 1998, <www.sierraclub.org/sierra/199811/second.asp>; viewed 24 October 2002.

80. Thomas Berry, "Ethics and Ecology," paper delivered to the Harvard Center on Environmental Values, 9 April 1996; see also Brian Swimme and Thomas Berry, *The Universe Story* (New York: Harper Collins, 1992), and Berry, op. cit. note 7.

Index

Other Worldwatch Papers

On Climate Change, Energy, and Materials

160: Reading the Weathervane: Climate Policy From Rio to Johannesburg, 2002

157: Hydrogen Futures: Toward a Sustainable Energy System, 2001

151: Micropower: The Next Electrical Era, 2000

149: Paper Cuts: Recovering the Paper Landscape, 1999

144: Mind Over Matter: Recasting the Role of Materials in Our Lives, 1998

138: Rising Sun, Gathering Winds: Policies To Stabilize the Climate and Strengthen Economies, 1997

130: Climate of Hope: New Strategies for Stabilizing the World's Atmosphere, 1996

On Ecological and Human Health

153: Why Poison Ourselves: A Precautionary Approach to Synthetic Chemicals, 2000

148: Nature's Cornucopia: Our Stakes in Plant Diversity, 1999

145: Safeguarding the Health of Oceans, 1999

142: Rocking the Boat: Conserving Fisheries and Protecting Jobs, 1998

141: Losing Strands in the Web of Life: Vertebrate Declines and the Conservation of Biological Diversity, 1998

140: Taking a Stand: Cultivating a New Relationship With the World's Forests, 1998

129: Infecting Ourselves: How Environmental and Social Disruptions Trigger Disease, 1996

On Economics, Institutions, and Security

162: The Anatomy of Resource Wars, 2002

159: Traveling Light: New Paths for International Tourism, 2001

158: Unnatural Disasters, 2001

155: Still Waiting for the Jubilee: Pragmatic Solutions for the Third World Debt Crisis, 2001

152: Working for the Environment: A Growing Source of Jobs, 2000

146: Ending Violent Conflict, 1999

139: Investing in the Future: Harnessing Private Capital Flows for Environmentally Sustainable Development, 1998

On Food, Water, Population, and Urbanization

163: Home Grown: The Case for Local Food in a Global Market, 2002

161: Correcting Gender Myopia: Gender Equity, Women's Welfare, and the Environment, 2002

156: City Limits: Putting the Brakes on Sprawl, 2001

154: Deep Trouble: The Hidden Threat of Groundwater Pollution, 2000

150: Underfed and Overfed: The Global Epidemic of Malnutrition, 2000

147: Reinventing Cities for People and the Planet, 1999

136: The Agricultural Link: How Environmental Deterioration Could Disrupt Economic Progress, 1997

Other Publications From the Worldwatch Institute

State of the World 2003   *Available January 2003*
Worldwatch's flagship annual is used by government officials, corporate
planners, journalists, development specialists, professors, students,
and concerned citizens in over 120 countries. Published in more than
20 different languages, it is one of the most widely used resources for
analysis.

State of the World Library 2003
Subscribe to the *State of the World Library* and join thousands of
decisionmakers and concerned citizens who stay current on emerging
environmental issues. The *State of the World Library* includes
Worldwatch's flagship annuals, *State of the World* and *Vital Signs*, plus
all four of the highly readable, up-to-date, and authoritative *Worldwatch
Papers* as they are published throughout the calendar year.

Signposts 2002
This CD-ROM provides instant, searchable access to over 965 pages of
full text from the last two editions of *State of the World* and *Vital Signs*,
comprehensive data sets going back as far as 50 years, and easy-to-
understand graphs and tables. Fully indexed, *Signposts 2002* contains
a powerful search engine for effortless search and retrieval. Plus, it is
platform independent and fully compatible with all Windows (3.1 and
up), Macintosh, and Unix/Linux operating systems.

Vital Signs 2002
Written by Worldwatch's team of researchers, this annual provides comprehensive, user-friendly information on key trends and includes tables
and graphs that help readers assess the developments that are changing
their lives for better or for worse.

World Watch
This award-winning bimonthly magazine is internationally recognized
for the clarity and comprehensiveness of its articles on global trends.
Keep up to speed on the latest developments in population growth,
climate change, species extinction, and the rise of new forms of human
behavior and governance.

*To make a tax-deductible contribution or to order any of Worldwatch's
publications, call us toll-free at 888-544-2303 (or 570-320-2076 outside
the U.S.), fax us at 570-322-2063, e-mail us at wwpub@worldwatch.org,
or visit our website at www.worldwatch.org.*